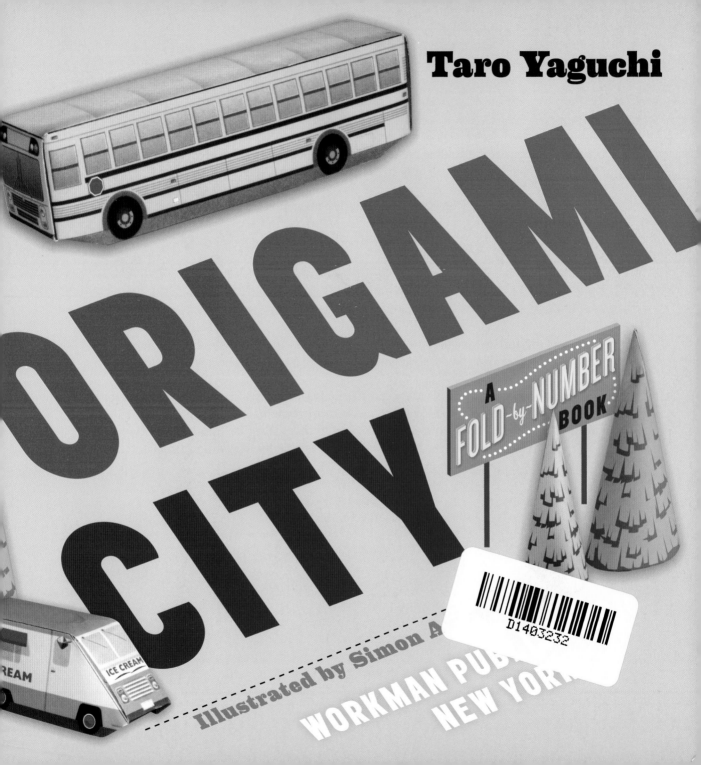

Taro Yaguchi

ORIGAMI CITY

A FOLD-by-NUMBER BOOK

Illustrated by Simon A.

WORKMAN PUBLISHING
NEW YORK

Library of Congress Cataloging-in-Publication Data is available.

ISBN 978-0-7611-8927-5

Design by Sara Corbett
Illustrations by Simon Arizpe
Technical illustrations by Taro Yaguchi

Taro's Origami Studio would like to give special thanks to Frank Ling for his help with conceptualizing and designing, and to Ben Friesen for his help with editing.

Workman books are available at special discounts when purchased in bulk for premiums and sales promotions as well as for fund-raising or educational use. Special editions or book excerpts can also be created to specification. For details, contact the Special Sales Director at the address below or send an email to specialmarkets@workman.com.

Workman Publishing Co., Inc.
225 Varick Street
New York, NY 10014-4381

workman.com

WORKMAN is a registered trademark of Workman Publishing Co., Inc.

Printed in China
First printing May 2020

10 9 8 7 6 5 4 3 2 1

Contents

Welcome to Origami City!

This city is *yours*! You get to design it, build it, and make it your own. Do you want the ice cream shop to be right next to the school? Go for it—it's up to you! Read on to learn all the things you should keep in mind as you build and explore your new city . . .

Parts of This Kit

Your Origami City kit is packed full of fun. It includes:

• **This book**, which has step-by-step diagrams for each origami model you can fold to build your city. You will find instructions for all the things your bustling city might need, from a hardworking dump truck to a trusty golden retriever!

• **A foldout paper mat** to give your city a foundation to build on. It has streets, plus open areas where you can arrange folded stoplights, buildings, and vehicles—and move them around—in whatever way you choose!

• **104 folding papers**, specially designed to fold each model in your city. Look for them in the envelope with the foldout mat, and make sure you use the right paper (or papers) for each model! Note: Some small models are combined onto a single sheet, while other models require multiple sheets. Cut the pieces apart if needed before folding.

What Is Origami, Anyway?

Chances are you've heard of origami. It's the ancient art of paper folding that originated in either Japan or China—historians aren't totally sure! The word "origami" itself comes from the Japanese words *oru*, meaning "to fold" and *kami*, meaning "paper." Traditional origami techniques use one square piece of paper, and the models are created without any cutting or gluing! But some modern origami styles have changed these rules a bit.

What Is Fold-by-Number Origami?

This book introduces you to my patented Fold-by-Number technique, which will help you to fold complex models more easily. It uses lined, numbered folding sheets so you know exactly where and when to make the folds.

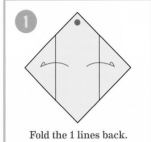

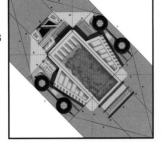

Fold the 1 lines back.

Each line is numbered in the order it should be folded and corresponds with a step in the written instructions in this book. It's easy! Step 1 shows you how to fold line 1 on the folding sheet. Step 2 shows you what to do with line 2, and so on.

Unlike in traditional origami, sometimes you will cut the folding sheets before you begin folding. This is to help the shapes look realistic and give your city a super polished look! For those projects you will need a pair of scissors. Look for the scissor symbol on the folding papers to show you where to cut. ✂

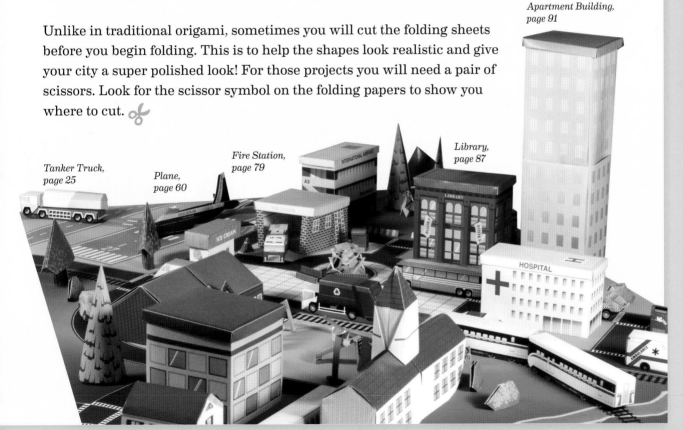

Apartment Building, page 91

Library, page 87

Fire Station, page 79

Tanker Truck, page 25

Plane, page 60

How to Use This Book

This book is organized into categories: If you want to fold a car, look for it in the Vehicles section. If you want to fold a chipmunk, it will be in the Animals section with the dog and the rabbit! Check out the table of contents on page iii for all of the categories and a list of all the projects.

Some projects are harder than others. But don't worry! We will help you figure out where to start. Each model is ranked in a 4-star rating system. (Look for it on the first page of each project.)

★☆☆☆   This model is pretty simple—start there!

★★☆☆   It's a little more complex, but nothing you can't handle!

★★★☆   The model is complicated and might be a challenge, but don't worry—you got this!

★★★★   The model is extra hard, so don't get frustrated if it takes you a few tries.

Work your way up, and if a model is too tricky (even if it has a 1-star rating), don't be afraid to ask for help. Sometimes it's easier to work on them with friends!

Evergreen Tree, page 134

Streetlamp, page 116

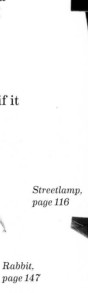

Rabbit, page 147

Bush, page 136

Chipmunk, page 145

Tips and Tricks to Fold-by-Number

Check the level of each project here.

This scissor icon lets you know you need to cut out the paper before you fold.

Check how many folding papers you need for each project before you start folding.

Make sure you have the right folding paper and that it's oriented correctly before you start folding.

MAIL TRUCK LEVEL ★★★★

Mail trucks deliver mail from the post office, and pick up letters and packages that have been dropped in mailboxes. They make stops at personal mailboxes (page 110) and at public mailboxes (page 108) where anyone can drop letters to be mailed. **Number of Folding Papers: 1**

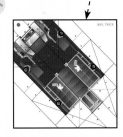

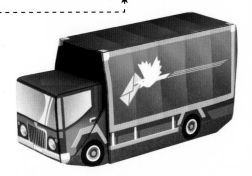

1

Fold the 1 lines back.

Fold-by-Number Symbols

There are many symbols used in origami, but these are the ones you need to complete the projects in *this* book.

Traffic Cone, page 130

A **solid line** tells you to fold back, creating a convex fold, like a mountain peak. (In traditional origami this is called a mountain fold.)

A **dotted line** tells you to fold forward, creating a concave fold, like a valley. (In traditional origami this is called a valley fold.)

This arrow tells you to **fold back**.

This arrow tells you to **fold forward**.

This arrow tells you to **fold back and unfold**, leaving a crease.

This arrow tells you to **fold forward and unfold**, leaving a crease.

Train, page 9

Red Dot Almost every folding sheet has a red dot on it to help you orient the project. Match it to the red dot on the instruction diagrams to make sure your project is pointing in the right direction when you fold.

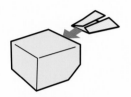

Collapse This red arrow tells you to push in part of the model, to give it shape.

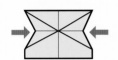

Insert This green arrow shows you how to fit models together when a project has more than one piece.

Basketball Hoop, page 120

Flip This arrow tells you to flip the model over.

Rotate This arrow tells you to turn your model 90 or 180 degrees.

Tape It's rare, but this symbol tells you where and when to use tape to assemble a project with more than one piece.

Don't Forget:

1. Fold in order. Start with line 1, and go from there.

2. Look for the red dot (see page ix). Make sure as you're following along with the instructions that your model is pointing in the right direction.

3. Check how many sheets a project needs, and that you grabbed the right ones.

4. Look for the scissor symbol to know where to make cuts.

5. If you get confused, don't worry! Ask for help, check the symbol key, or take a break and try a simpler project.

6. Don't forget to play! After you fold, pull out the paper play mat and build your city, exactly how you want it.

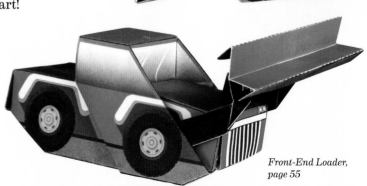

Excavator, page 51

You're Ready!

Now that you've read through these tips, tricks, and secrets, you're ready to start! What will you make first?

Happy folding,

矢口太邻

Taro Yaguchi

Front-End Loader, page 55

SCHOOL BUS, CITY BUS, AND COACH

Buses transport many people at once, so they are an essential part of any city. School buses take students to school (page 75). City buses make local stops around town. Coach buses take people on long-distance trips, often across city or state lines. They might not be headed to the same places, but you can use the same steps to fold each kind of bus. **Number of Folding Papers: 1**

1 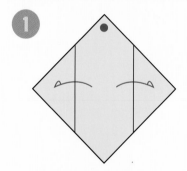 Fold the 1 lines back.	**2** 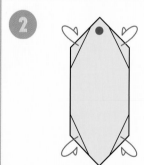 Fold the 2 lines back.
3 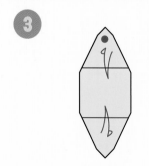 Fold the 3 lines back and unfold.	**4** 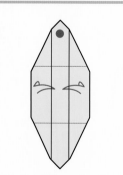 Fold the 4 lines back and unfold.

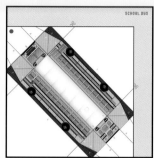

SCHOOL BUS

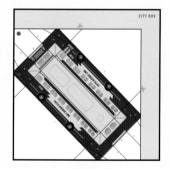

CITY BUS

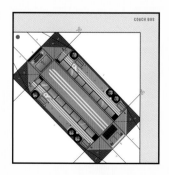

COACH BUS

5

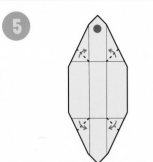

Fold the 5 lines, bringing lines 3 and 4 together, collapsing the model as shown.

6

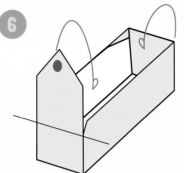
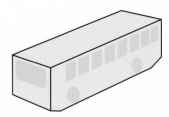

Fold the 6 lines back, tucking the flaps in and under to lock the sides.

ICE CREAM TRUCK and AMBULANCE

Ambulances and ice cream trucks serve very different purposes, but in origami, they are folded in the same way. Once you've folded them, park the ambulance near the hospital (page 100) and plan out the ice cream truck route. You can make the sound effects yourself! **Number of Folding Papers: 1**

ICE CREAM TRUCK

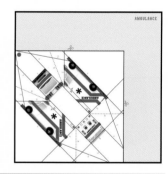
AMBULANCE

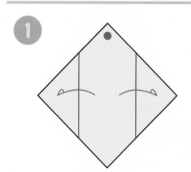

1 Fold the 1 lines back.

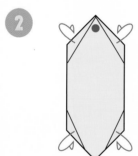

2 Fold the 2 lines back.

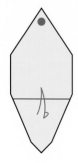

3 Fold line 3 back and unfold.

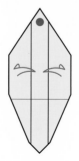

4 Fold the 4 lines back and unfold.

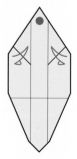

5 Fold the 5 lines back and unfold.

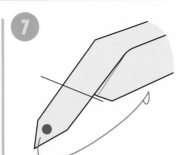

6

Fold the 6 lines, bringing lines 4 and 5 together.

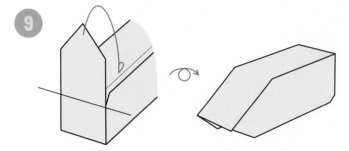

7

Fold line 7 back, tucking the flap in and under to lock the sides. Rotate the model.

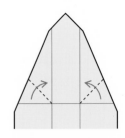

8

Fold the 8 lines.

9

Fold line 9 back, tucking the flap in and under to lock the sides. Flip the model over.

MAIL TRUCK LEVEL ★★☆☆

Mail trucks deliver mail from the post office, and pick up letters and packages that have been dropped in mailboxes. They make stops at personal mailboxes (page 110) and at public mailboxes (page 108) where anyone can drop letters to be mailed. **Number of Folding Papers: 1**

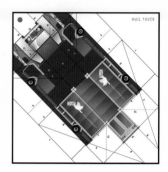

 1

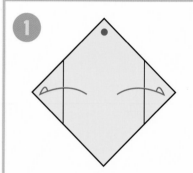

Fold the 1 lines back.

 2

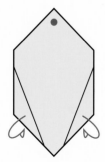

Fold the 2 lines back.

3

Fold the 3 lines back and unfold.

4

Fold line 4 back and unfold.

5

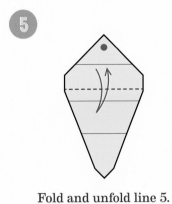

Fold and unfold line 5.

6

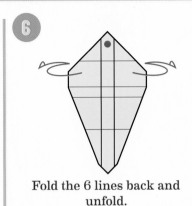

Fold the 6 lines back and unfold.

7

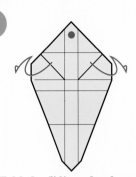

Fold the 7 lines back and unfold.

8

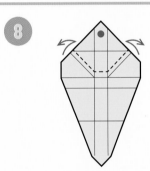 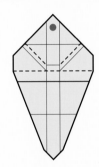 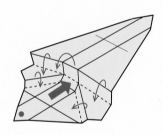 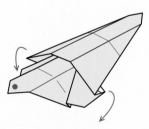

Fold and unfold the 8 lines. Refold lines 4, 5, 7, and 8, collapsing the model as shown.

9

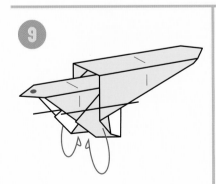

Fold the 9 lines back.

10

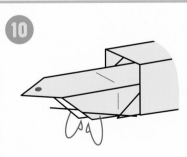

Fold the 10 lines back.

11

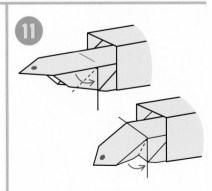

Fold the 11 lines.

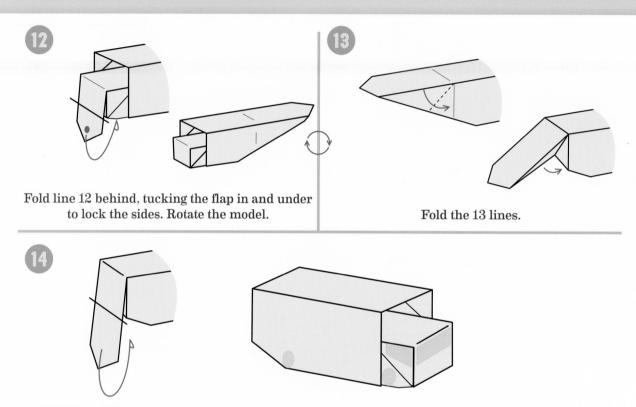

12 Fold line 12 behind, tucking the flap in and under to lock the sides. Rotate the model.

13 Fold the 13 lines.

14 Fold line 14 back, tucking the flap in and under to lock the sides.

TRAIN ENGINE AND CAR LEVEL ★★★★

All aboard! Trains are a great way to travel if you want to look out the window and see the world unfold around you. Make sure the trains passing through your city let everyone know they're rumbling by with a loud whistle!

Number of Folding Papers: 2

TRAIN ENGINE

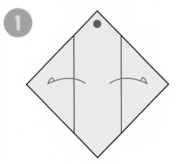
Fold the 1 lines back.

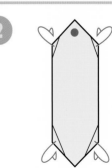
Fold the 2 lines back.

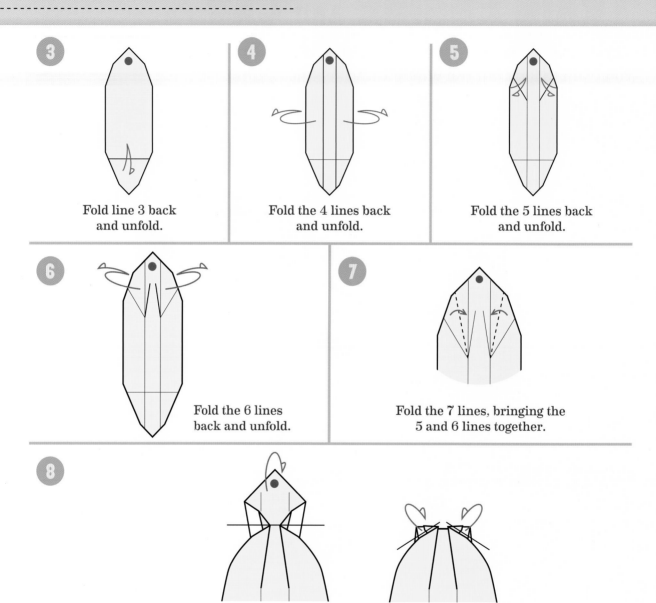

3 Fold line 3 back and unfold.

4 Fold the 4 lines back and unfold.

5 Fold the 5 lines back and unfold.

6 Fold the 6 lines back and unfold.

7 Fold the 7 lines, bringing the 5 and 6 lines together.

8 Fold line 8 back, tucking the flap inside. This will leave two little triangles poking out. Fold those two triangles back, tucking the flap inside.

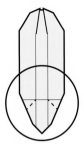 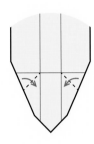

Fold the 9 lines.

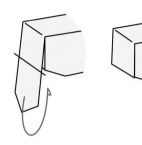

Fold line 10 back, tucking the flap in and under to lock the sides.

 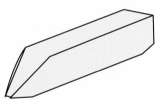

Rotate the model and set it aside to fold the train car.

TRAIN CAR

Fold the 1 lines back.

 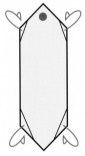

Fold the 2 lines back.

Fold the 3 lines back and unfold.

  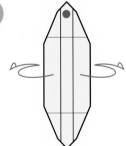

Fold the 4 lines back and unfold.

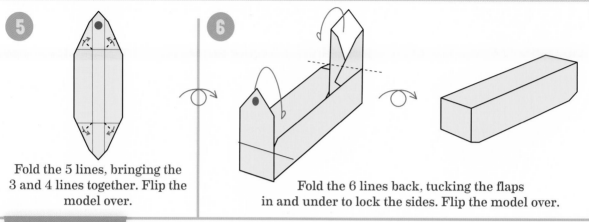

5 Fold the 5 lines, bringing the 3 and 4 lines together. Flip the model over.

6 Fold the 6 lines back, tucking the flaps in and under to lock the sides. Flip the model over.

ASSEMBLY

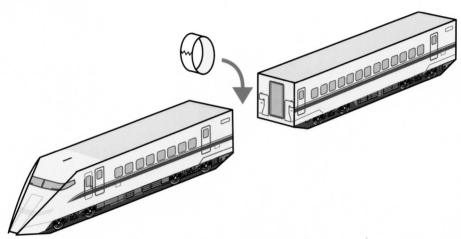

To assemble, insert a loop of tape between the back of the engine and the front of the train car.

CAR, TAXI, AND POLICE CAR LEVEL ★★★☆

You can use the same steps to fold the car that you use to fold the taxi or the police car. Fold them all (in different colors!) and place them around your busy city. Help regulate traffic flow by placing traffic lights (page 112) at busy intersections and setting up streetlamps (page 116) so nighttime drivers can see where they are going. **Number of Folding Papers: 1**

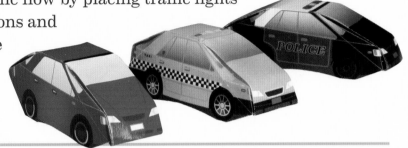

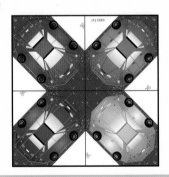
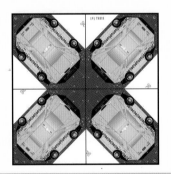
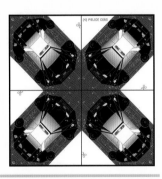

1

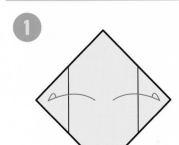

Fold the 1 lines back.

2

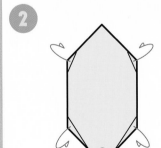

Fold the 2 lines back.

3

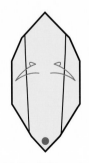

Fold the 3 lines back and unfold.

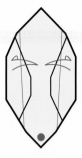

Fold the 4 lines back and unfold.

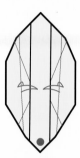

Fold the 5 lines back and unfold.

Fold the 6 lines, lining them up with the 4 lines, collapsing the model.

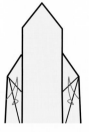

Fold the 7 lines back and unfold.

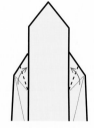

Fold the 8 lines, bringing the short 7 lines to the 6 lines, collapsing as shown.

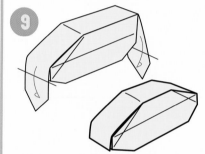

Fold the 9 lines back, tucking and locking the flaps.

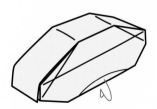
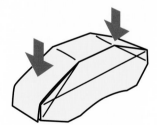
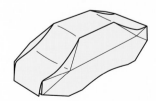

Fold the 10 lines back. Press gently down where the windshield meets the hood.

LIMOUSINE LEVEL ★★★☆

People rent limousines when a big group has a fancy place to go. Where is this limo headed? To pick up high schoolers taking prom pictures at the park (page 127)? Or maybe it's escorting a movie star to the airport (page 96) to catch a flight? **Number of Folding Papers: 1**

LIMOUSINE

1

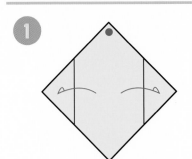

Fold the 1 lines back.

2

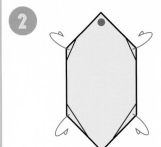

Fold the 2 lines back.

3

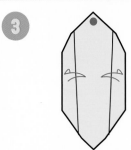

Fold the 3 lines back and unfold.

4

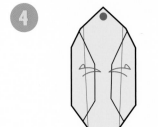

Fold the 4 lines back and unfold.

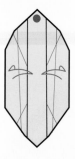

Fold the 5 lines
back and unfold.

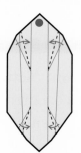

Fold the 6 lines, collapsing
the model so that lines
4 and 5 align.

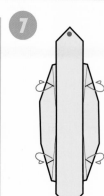

Fold the 7
lines back.

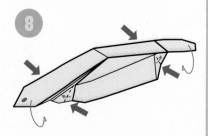

Fold the 8 lines, collapsing
the corners as shown so that
lines 4 and 7 align.

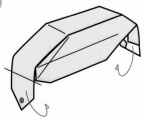

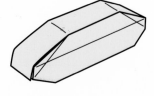

Fold the 9 lines back, tucking and locking the sides.

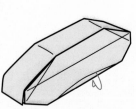

Fold the 10 lines back.

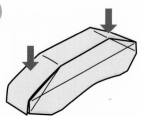

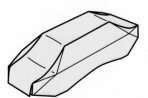

Gently press down on the windshield and
rear window to complete the model.

SPORTS CAR LEVEL ★★★★

This is a type of Italian sports car called a Lamborghini. It's known for being super sleek and super fast. Can you find a place for one in your city?

Number of Folding Papers: 1

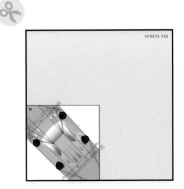

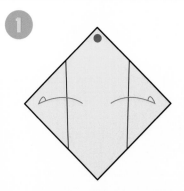

Fold the 1 lines back.

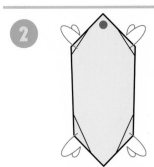

Fold the 2 lines back.

Fold the 3 lines back and unfold.

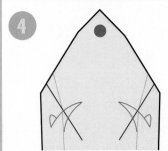

Fold the 4 lines back and unfold.

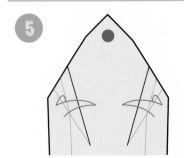

Fold the 5 lines back and unfold.

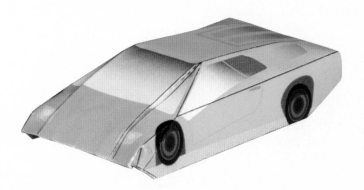

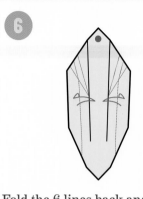

6 Fold the 6 lines back and unfold.

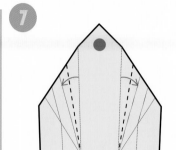

7 Fold the 7 lines, bringing lines 6 and 5 together.

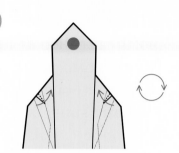

8 Fold the 8 lines, collapsing the corners as shown. Rotate the model.

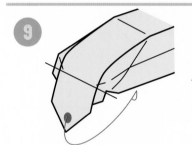

9 Fold line 9 back, tucking and locking the sides. Rotate the model.

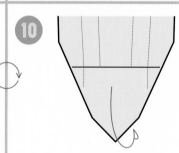

10 Fold line 10 back and unfold.

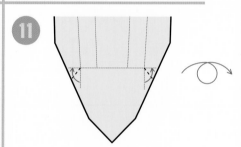

11 Fold the 11 lines, collapsing the corners. Flip the model over.

12

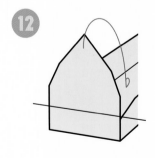  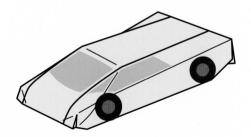

Fold line 12 back, tucking and locking the sides. Flip the model over.

SUV LEVEL ★★★☆

SUV stands for Sport Utility Vehicle. SUVs are larger than regular cars, and they are better at driving across rocky terrain or off-road! Drive your SUV out of the city and into nature!

Number of Folding Papers: 1

 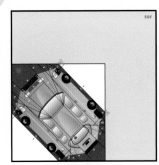

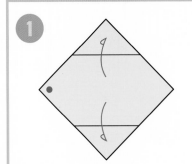

Fold the 1 lines back.

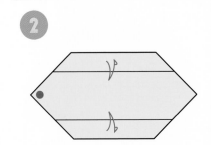

Fold the 2 lines back and unfold.

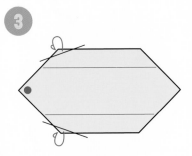

Fold the 3 lines back.

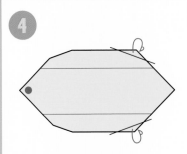

Fold the 4 lines back.

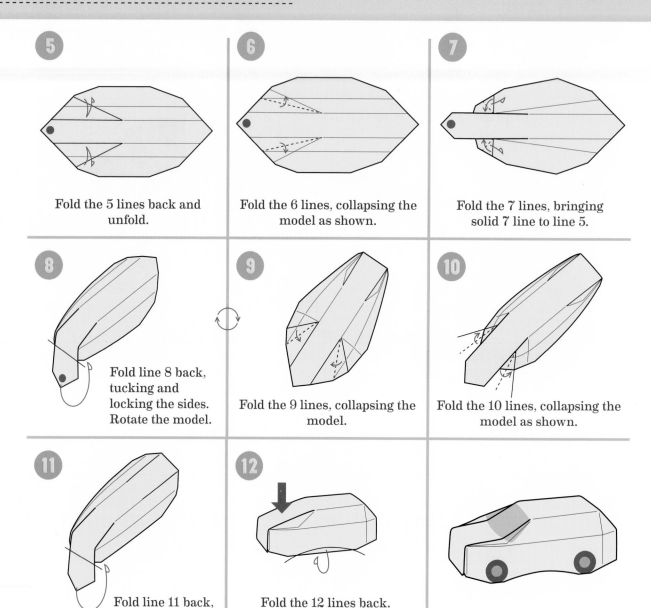

5 Fold the 5 lines back and unfold.

6 Fold the 6 lines, collapsing the model as shown.

7 Fold the 7 lines, bringing solid 7 line to line 5.

8 Fold line 8 back, tucking and locking the sides. Rotate the model.

9 Fold the 9 lines, collapsing the model.

10 Fold the 10 lines, collapsing the model as shown.

11 Fold line 11 back, tucking and locking the sides.

12 Fold the 12 lines back. Press down gently where the windshield meets the hood.

PUMPER FIRE ENGINE LEVEL ★★★★

Pumper trucks are equipped with hoses that connect to fire hydrants and pump water to put out fires. Pumpers work with hook and ladder trucks (page 46) to fight fires in your city! When they're not dowsing flames, you can find them parked inside the fire station (page 79).

Number of Folding Papers: 1

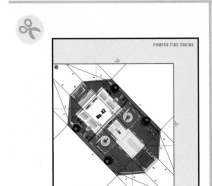

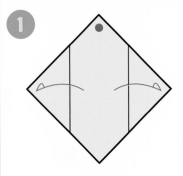
Fold the 1 lines back.

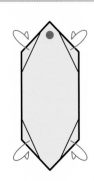
Fold the 2 lines back.

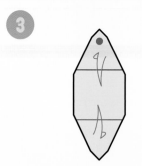

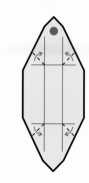

Fold the 3 lines back and unfold.

Fold the 4 lines back and unfold.

Fold the 5 lines.

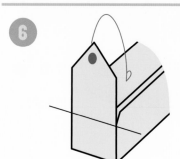

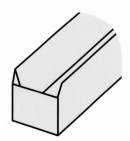

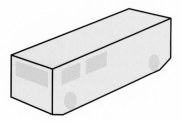

Fold the 6 lines back, tucking the flap in and under to lock the sides.

BIG DUMP TRUCK

Warm up your folding skills with this extra-large dump truck that you can make in just six steps with a single sheet of folding paper. Then test your skills on the small dump truck (page 31) that is constructed with two sheets of folding papers.

Number of Folding Papers: 1

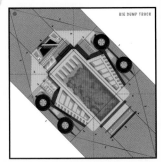

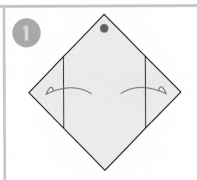

Fold the 1 lines back.

Fold the 2 lines back.

3

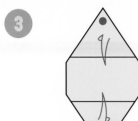

Fold the 3 lines back
and unfold.

4

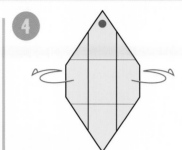

Fold the 4 lines back
and unfold.

5

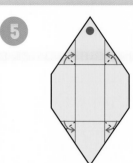

Fold the 5 lines, bringing lines
3 and 4 together, collapsing the
model.

6

  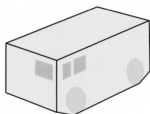

Fold the 6 line back, tucking the flap in and under to lock the sides. Flip the model over.

TANKER TRUCK LEVEL ★★☆☆

Tanker trucks are designed to carry liquids and gases. You can recognize a tanker truck by the shape of the tank it carries—a cylinder! This tanker truck might deliver gasoline to the airport (page 96) to fuel up the planes, or it could bring fresh water to the park, to pump into the fountain (page 128)!

Number of Folding Papers: 2

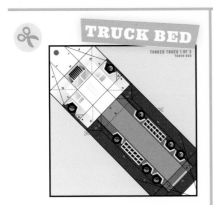

TRUCK BED

TANKER TRUCK 1 OF 2
TRUCK BED

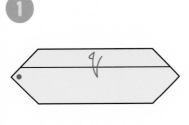

1

Fold line 1 back and unfold.

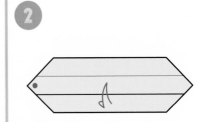

2

Fold line 2 back and unfold.

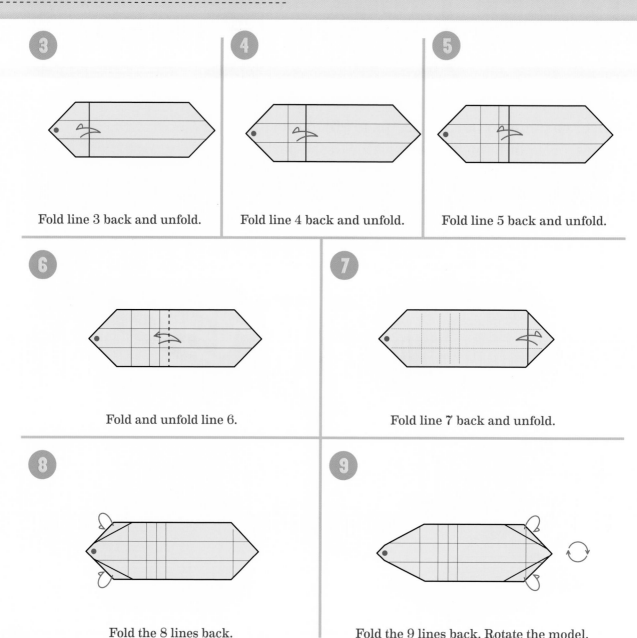

3

Fold line 3 back and unfold.

4

Fold line 4 back and unfold.

5

Fold line 5 back and unfold.

6

Fold and unfold line 6.

7

Fold line 7 back and unfold.

8

Fold the 8 lines back.

9

Fold the 9 lines back. Rotate the model.

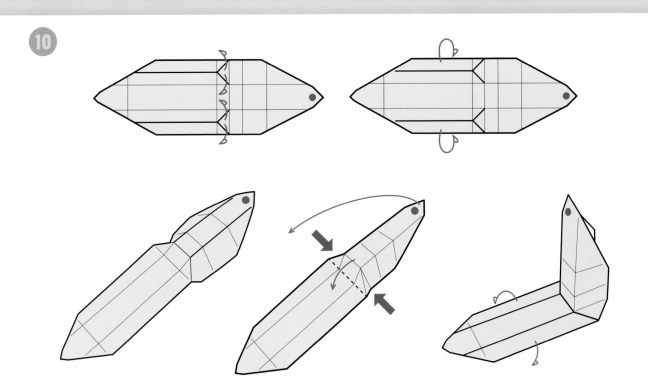

Fold the 10 lines back, refolding line 6 and collapsing the model as shown.

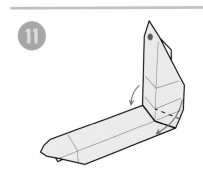

Fold the 11 lines.

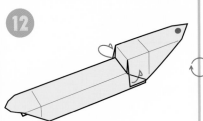

Fold the 12 lines back, tucking the flaps into the pockets behind the folds. Rotate the model.

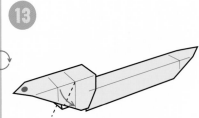

Fold the 13 lines, aligning lines 1 and 2 with the 3 lines on each side.

14

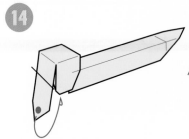

Fold line 14 back, tucking the flap and locking in the sides. Rotate the model.

15

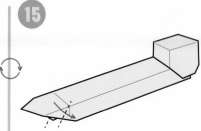

Fold the 15 lines, aligning folds 1 and 2 with the 7 fold on each side.

16

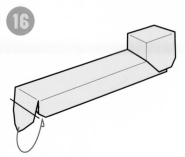

Fold line 16 back, tucking the flap and locking in the sides.

17

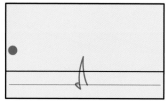

The bed of the truck is complete. Set it aside while you fold the tank.

TANK

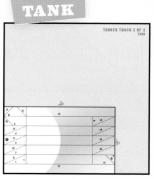

TANKER TRUCK 2 OF 2
TANK

1

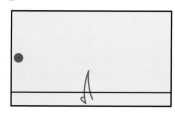

Fold line 1 back and unfold.

2

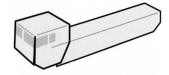

Fold line 2 back and unfold.

3

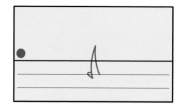

Fold line 3 back and unfold.

4

Fold line 4 back and unfold.

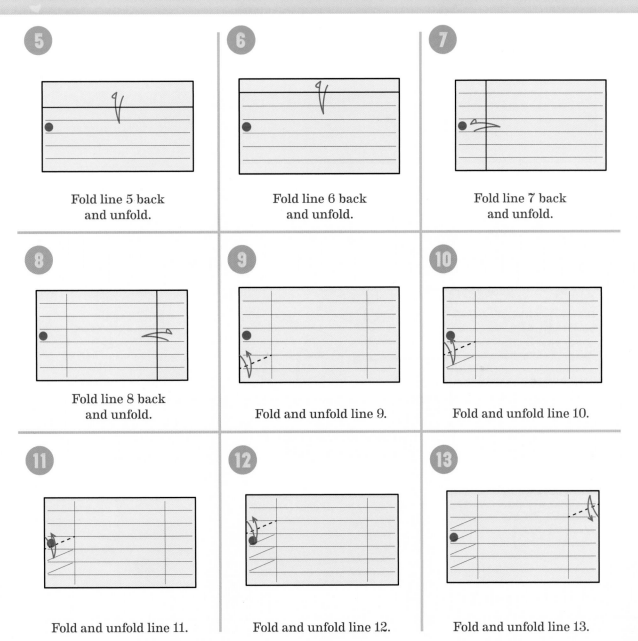

5

Fold line 5 back
and unfold.

6

Fold line 6 back
and unfold.

7

Fold line 7 back
and unfold.

8

Fold line 8 back
and unfold.

9

Fold and unfold line 9.

10

Fold and unfold line 10.

11

Fold and unfold line 11.

12

Fold and unfold line 12.

13

Fold and unfold line 13.

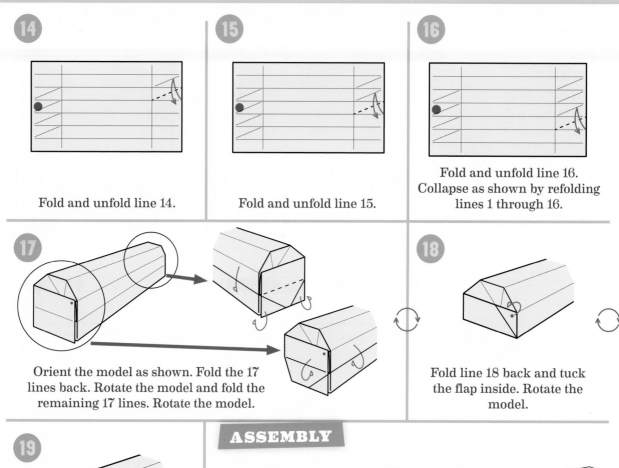

14 Fold and unfold line 14.

15 Fold and unfold line 15.

16 Fold and unfold line 16. Collapse as shown by refolding lines 1 through 16.

17 Orient the model as shown. Fold the 17 lines back. Rotate the model and fold the remaining 17 lines. Rotate the model.

18 Fold line 18 back and tuck the flap inside. Rotate the model.

19 Fold line 19 back, tucking the flap into the pocket. Refold line 6 to create a tab.

ASSEMBLY

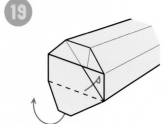

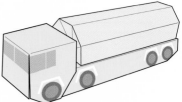

To assemble, insert the tab of the tank into the crease at the back of the truck cab.

SMALL DUMP TRUCK LEVEL ★★★★

Where is the construction happening in your city? Is the school (page 75) getting some brand-new classrooms, or is the park getting an awesome playground (page 120)? Wherever the construction is, this little dump truck will be a big help. A fun feature of this model is that once the cab and the truck bed are folded and assembled, the bed tips up like a real dump truck!

Number of Folding Papers: 2

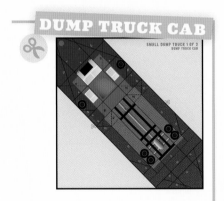

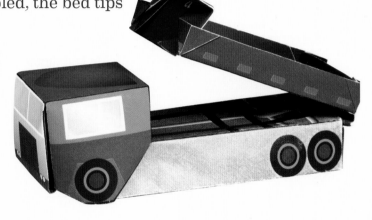

1

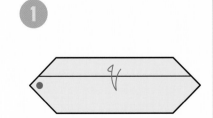

Fold line 1 back
and unfold.

2

Fold line 2 back
and unfold.

3

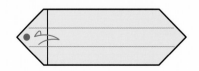

Fold line 3 back
and unfold.

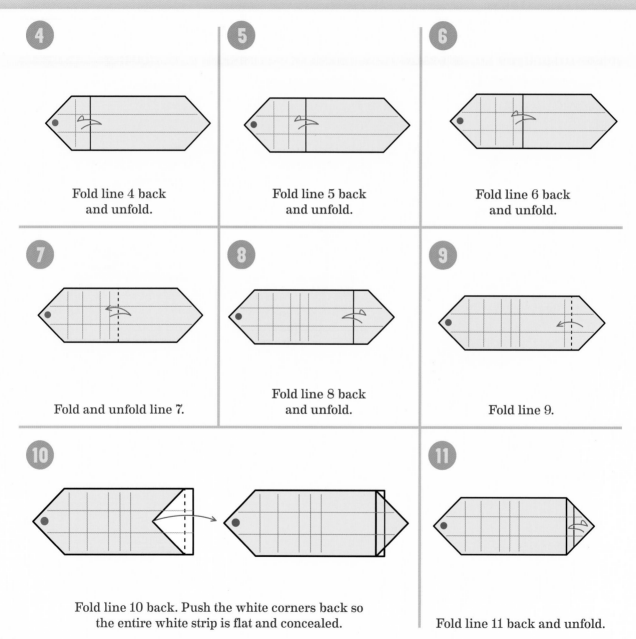

4

Fold line 4 back
and unfold.

5

Fold line 5 back
and unfold.

6

Fold line 6 back
and unfold.

7

Fold and unfold line 7.

8

Fold line 8 back
and unfold.

9

Fold line 9.

10

Fold line 10 back. Push the white corners back so
the entire white strip is flat and concealed.

11

Fold line 11 back and unfold.

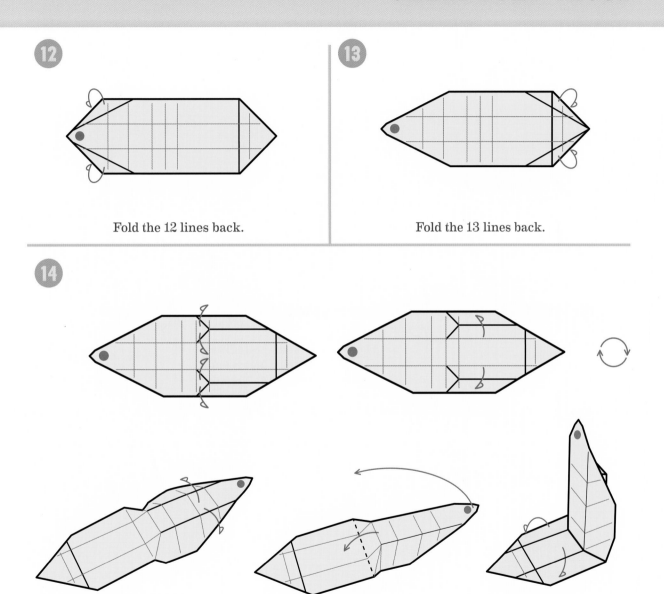

Fold the 12 lines back.

Fold the 13 lines back.

Fold the 14 lines back. Rotate the model and refold lines 1, 2, and 7, collapsing the model as shown.

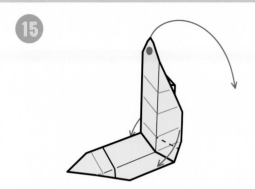

Fold the 15 lines, collapsing the model as shown.

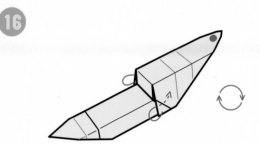

Fold the 16 lines back, tucking the flaps into the pocket to lock the sides in place. Rotate the model.

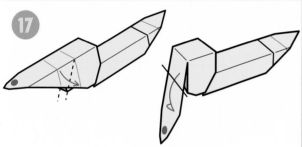

Fold the 17 lines. Refold line 3 back and tuck the flap inside. Rotate the model.

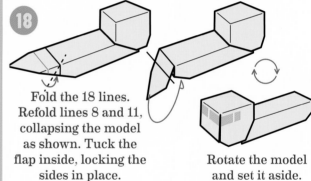

Fold the 18 lines. Refold lines 8 and 11, collapsing the model as shown. Tuck the flap inside, locking the sides in place.

Rotate the model and set it aside.

✂ DUMP TRUCK BED

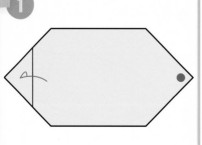

Fold line 1 back.

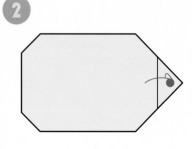

Fold line 2 back.

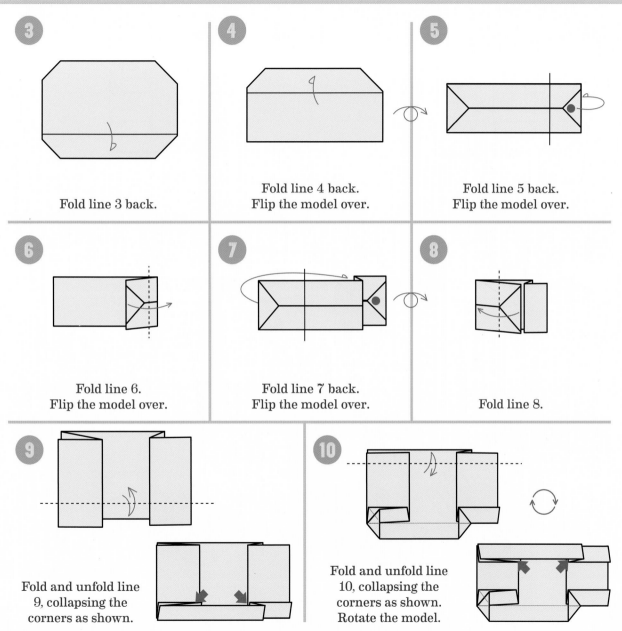

3 Fold line 3 back.

4 Fold line 4 back.
Flip the model over.

5 Fold line 5 back.
Flip the model over.

6 Fold line 6.
Flip the model over.

7 Fold line 7 back.
Flip the model over.

8 Fold line 8.

9 Fold and unfold line
9, collapsing the
corners as shown.

10 Fold and unfold line
10, collapsing the
corners as shown.
Rotate the model.

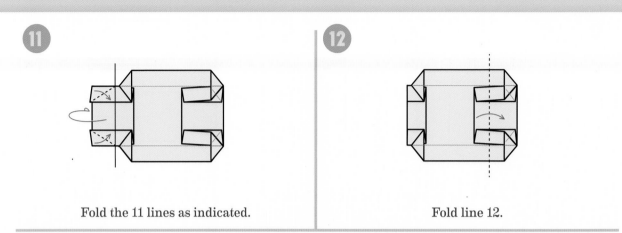

11 Fold the 11 lines as indicated.

12 Fold line 12.

13 Gently pull up the tabs and push in the sides as shown.

ASSEMBLY

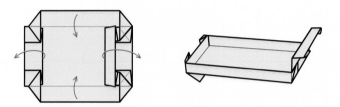

To assemble, insert the bottom tab of the dump truck bed (step 11) into the pocket at the back end of the dump truck cab.

TRACTOR TRAILER LEVEL ⭐⭐⭐⭐

Your city is busy and bustling with life! The tractor trailer will help deliver food and goods from other cities to the shops and restaurants where you live. What's inside this trailer? Boxes and boxes of books for the library (page 87)? Or maybe it's a refrigerated truck carrying hundreds of cartons of ice cream for the ice cream shop (page 83). Yum! **Number of Folding Papers: 2**

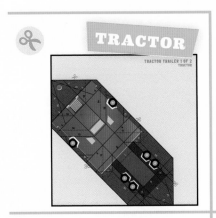

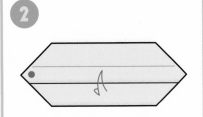

1

Fold line 1 back
and unfold.

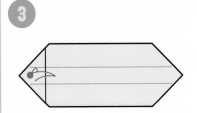

2

Fold line 2 back
and unfold.

3

Fold line 3 back
and unfold.

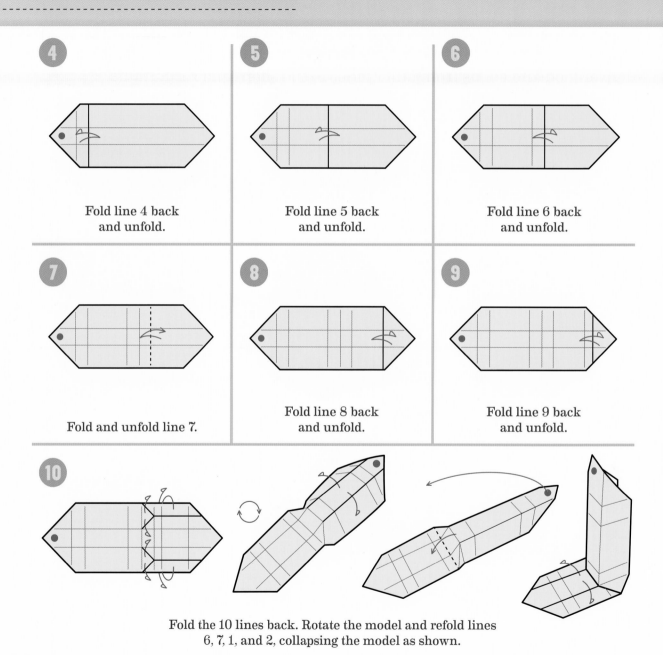

4 Fold line 4 back and unfold.

5 Fold line 5 back and unfold.

6 Fold line 6 back and unfold.

7 Fold and unfold line 7.

8 Fold line 8 back and unfold.

9 Fold line 9 back and unfold.

10 Fold the 10 lines back. Rotate the model and refold lines 6, 7, 1, and 2, collapsing the model as shown.

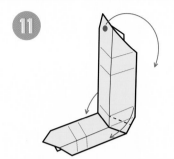

Fold the 11 lines, refolding the 5 lines, and collapsing the model as shown.

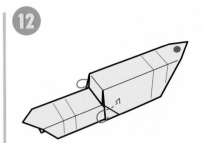

Fold the 12 lines back, tucking the flaps into the pocket to lock the sides in place.

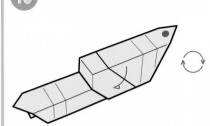

Fold the 13 lines back. Rotate the model.

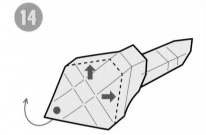

Fold the 14 lines. Refold lines 1 and 2, collapsing the model.

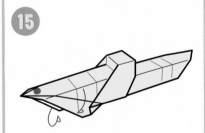

Fold the 15 lines back.

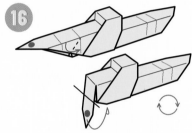

Fold the 16 lines. Refold line 3. Tuck the flap inside, locking the sides in place. Rotate the model.

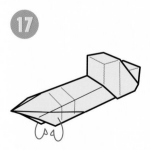

Fold the 17 lines back.

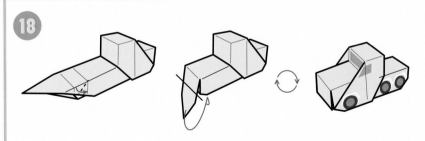

Fold the 18 lines. Refold lines 8 and 9, collapsing the model as shown. Tuck the flap inside, locking the sides in place. Rotate the model and set it aside.

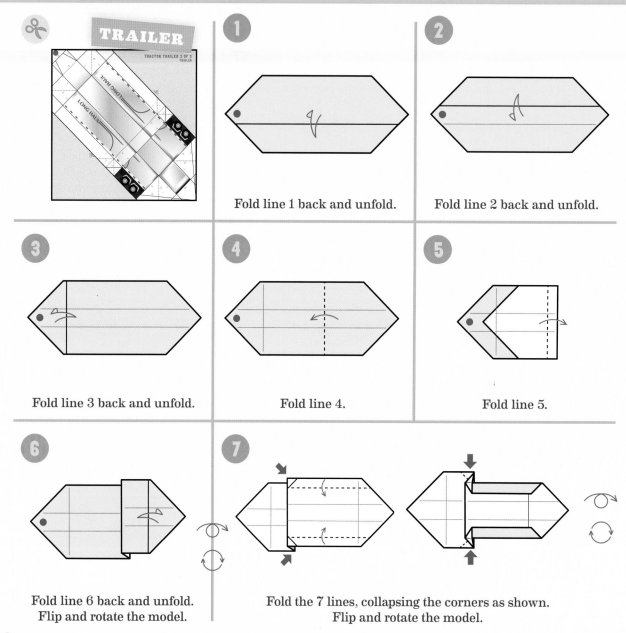

✂ TRAILER

TRACTOR TRAILER 2 OF 2
TRAILER

LONG HAUL

1

Fold line 1 back and unfold.

2

Fold line 2 back and unfold.

3

Fold line 3 back and unfold.

4

Fold line 4.

5

Fold line 5.

6

Fold line 6 back and unfold.
Flip and rotate the model.

7

Fold the 7 lines, collapsing the corners as shown.
Flip and rotate the model.

8

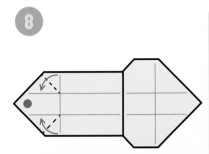

Fold the 8 lines. Refold lines
1 and 3 and lines 2 and 3,
collapsing the model as shown.

9

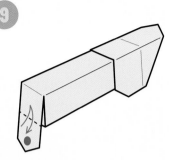

Fold and unfold line 9.

10

Fold line 10 back.

11

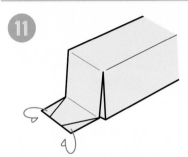

Fold the 11 lines back.
Rotate the model.

12

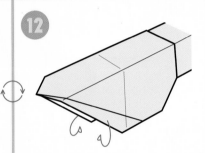

Fold the 12 lines back.

13

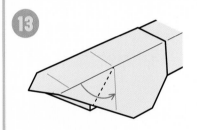

Fold the 13 lines, bringing lines
1 and 2 to line 6.

14

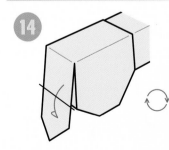

Fold line 14 back. Tuck the
flap inside, locking the sides in
place. Rotate the model.

ASSEMBLY

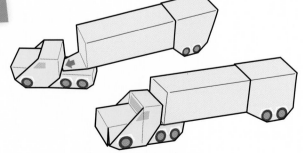

To assemble, insert the tab of the trailer into the
crease at the back of the truck cab.

GARBAGE TRUCK

LEVEL ★★★☆

Every city needs a garbage truck to keep it clean, transport the trash to a landfill, and ferry the recycling to a processing plant. Make sure this truck hits all the important stops—the garbage cans at the playground, the dumpster behind the school (page 75), and, of course, any construction sites! **Number of Folding Papers: 1**

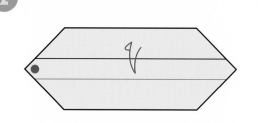

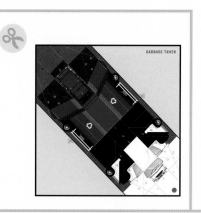

1

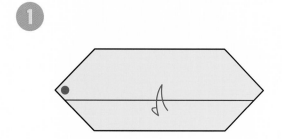

Fold line 1 back
and unfold.

2

Fold line 2 back
and unfold.

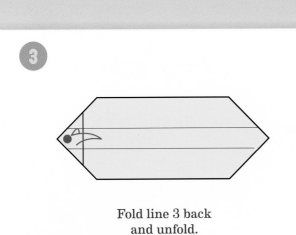

3

Fold line 3 back
and unfold.

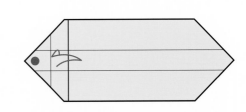

4

Fold line 4 back
and unfold.

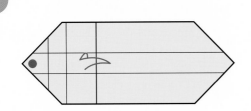

5

Fold line 5 back
and unfold.

6

Fold and unfold line 6.

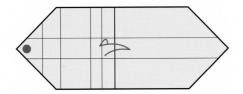

7

Fold line 7 back
and unfold.

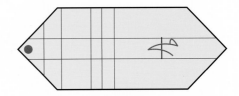

8

Fold line 8 back
and unfold.

 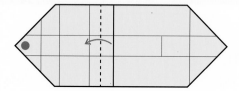

Fold line 9 back and unfold.
Refold lines 6 and 7 so that lines 5 and 7 line up.

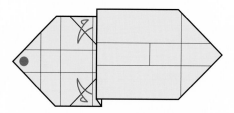

Unfold lines 6 and 7 slightly in order to fold
the 10 lines back, and unfold.

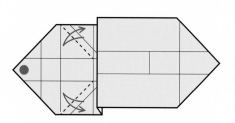 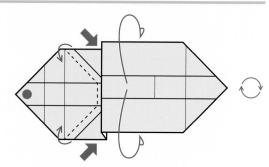

Fold the 11 lines. Refold the 10 lines and refold lines 1 and 2,
collapsing the model as shown. Rotate the model.

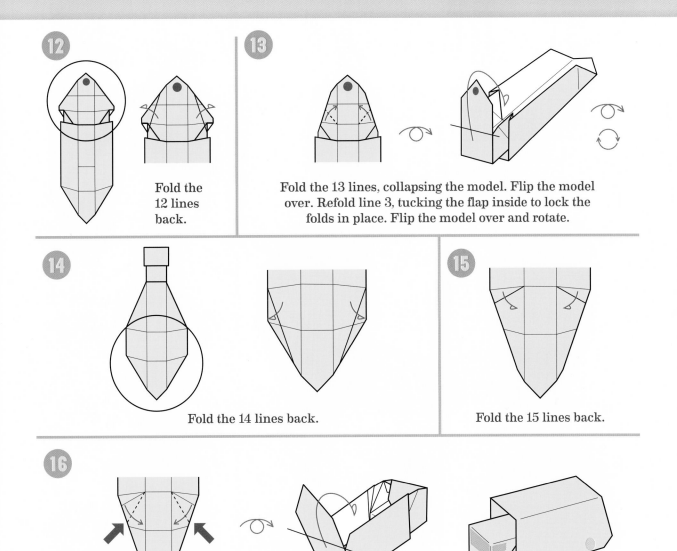

12 Fold the 12 lines back.

13 Fold the 13 lines, collapsing the model. Flip the model over. Refold line 3, tucking the flap inside to lock the folds in place. Flip the model over and rotate.

14 Fold the 14 lines back.

15 Fold the 15 lines back.

16 Fold the 16 lines, collapsing the model and bringing the 15 lines to meet the 1 and 2 lines. Flip the model over. Refold line 9, tucking the flap inside to lock the folds in place.

HOOK AND LADDER FIRE TRUCK

There are many kinds of fire trucks. Each one has an important role in a fire emergency. Hook and ladder trucks carry ladders and firefighters to the scene. Pumper trucks (page 21) bring the hoses and hook up to the fire hydrants to pump water.

Number of Folding Papers: 2

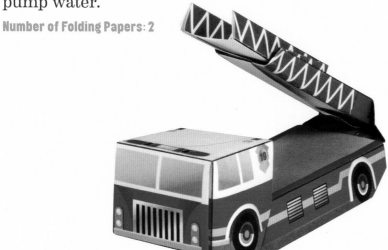

TRUCK

HOOK AND LADDER FIRE TRUCK 1 OF 2

1

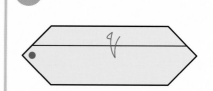

Fold line 1 back and unfold.

2

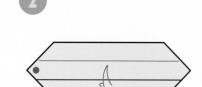

Fold line 2 back and unfold.

3

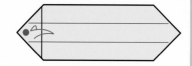

Fold line 3 back and unfold.

4

Fold line 4 back and unfold.

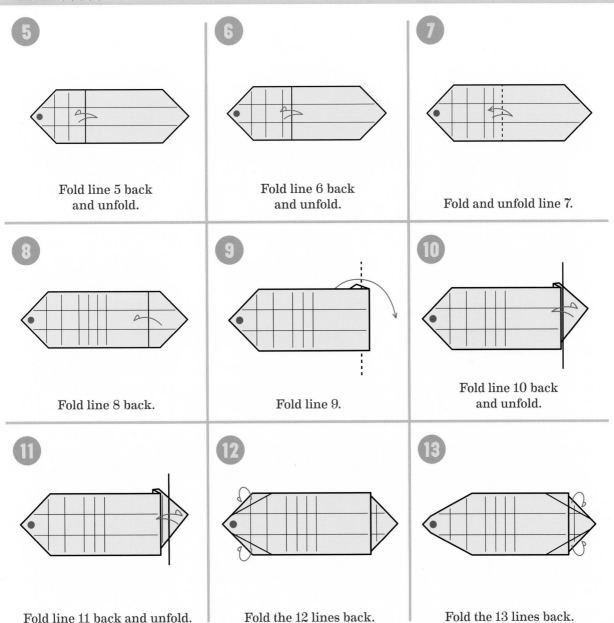

5 Fold line 5 back and unfold.

6 Fold line 6 back and unfold.

7 Fold and unfold line 7.

8 Fold line 8 back.

9 Fold line 9.

10 Fold line 10 back and unfold.

11 Fold line 11 back and unfold.

12 Fold the 12 lines back.

13 Fold the 13 lines back.

14

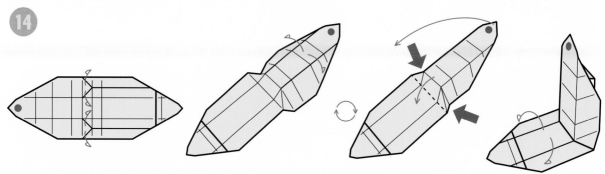

Fold the 14 lines back. Rotate the model. Refold lines 6 and
7, collapsing the model as shown. Refold lines 1 and 2.

15

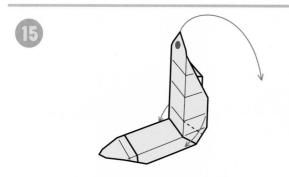

Fold the 15 lines, refolding line 5.

16

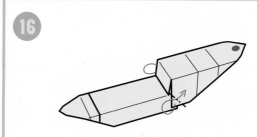

Fold the 16 lines back. Tuck the flaps to lock
the sides. Rotate the model.

17

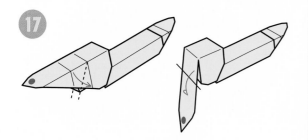

Fold the 17 lines, refolding line 4 and lines 1 and
2. Fold line 3, tucking the flap to lock the sides.
Rotate the model.

18

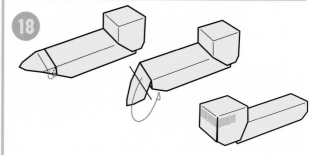

Fold the 18 lines, refolding line 9.
Refold line 11, tucking the flap to lock the sides.
Rotate the model and set it aside.

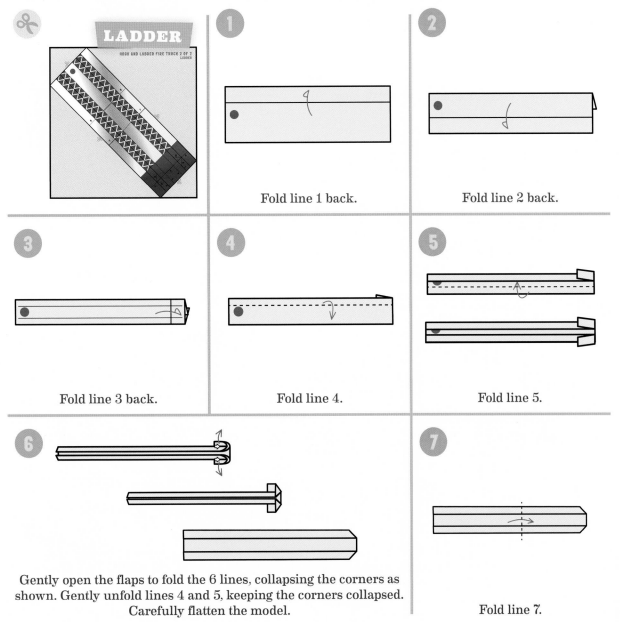

1 Fold line 1 back.

2 Fold line 2 back.

3 Fold line 3 back.

4 Fold line 4.

5 Fold line 5.

6 Gently open the flaps to fold the 6 lines, collapsing the corners as shown. Gently unfold lines 4 and 5, keeping the corners collapsed. Carefully flatten the model.

7 Fold line 7.

49

Fold line 8. Refold lines 4 and 5. Rotate the model.

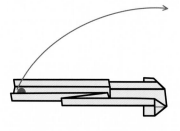 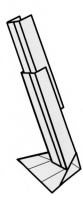

ASSEMBLY

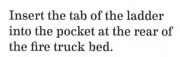

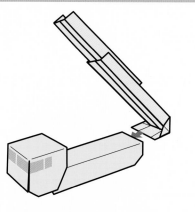 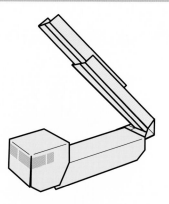

Insert the tab of the ladder into the pocket at the rear of the fire truck bed.

EXCAVATOR LEVEL ★★★☆

Time to dig! The excavator and its long, strong arm can dig out foundations for houses (page 65), and help smooth out land for new roads. Send this excavator where your city needs it most.

Number of Folding Papers: 1

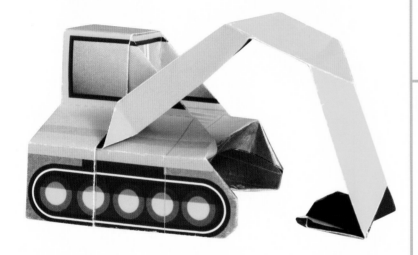

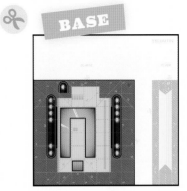

BASE

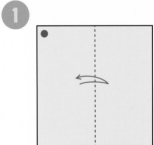

1

Fold and unfold line 1.

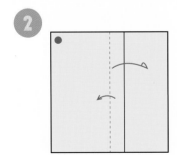

2

Fold line 2 back.
Refold line 1.

3

Fold line 3 back and unfold.

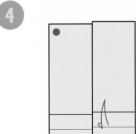

4

Fold line 4 back and unfold.

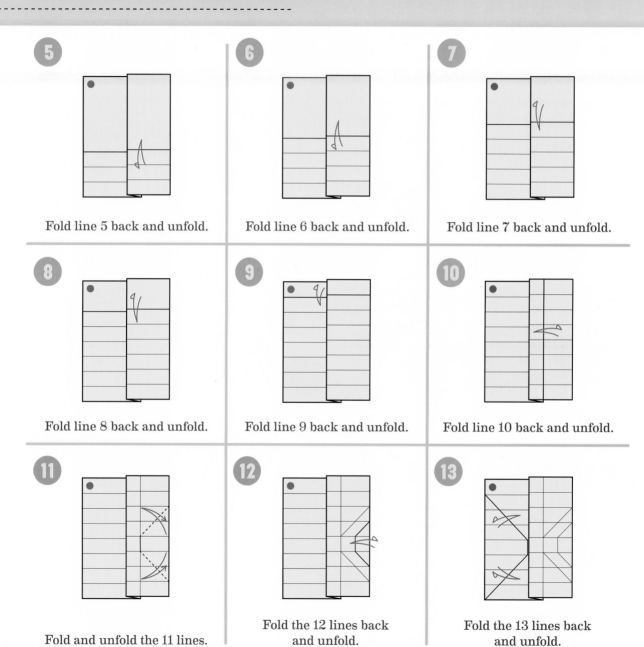

5 Fold line 5 back and unfold.

6 Fold line 6 back and unfold.

7 Fold line 7 back and unfold.

8 Fold line 8 back and unfold.

9 Fold line 9 back and unfold.

10 Fold line 10 back and unfold.

11 Fold and unfold the 11 lines.

12 Fold the 12 lines back and unfold.

13 Fold the 13 lines back and unfold.

14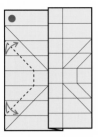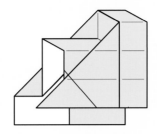

Fold and unfold the 14 lines. Assemble as shown by refolding lines 11, 12, 13, 14, 5, and 6.

15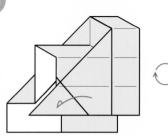

Fold line 15 back, tucking the flap inside. Rotate the model.

16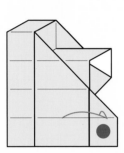

Fold line 16 back.

17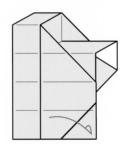

Fold line 17 back. Rotate the model.

18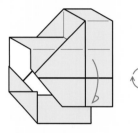

Fold line 18 back, creasing and gently unfolding to sit flat. Rotate the model.

19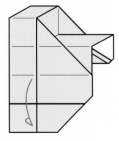

Fold line 19 back, creasing and gently unfolding to sit flat.

 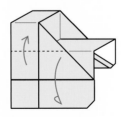

Fold line 8 back. Fold line 7 forward.

20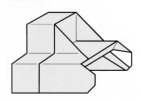

Fold line 20 back. Set aside excavator base.

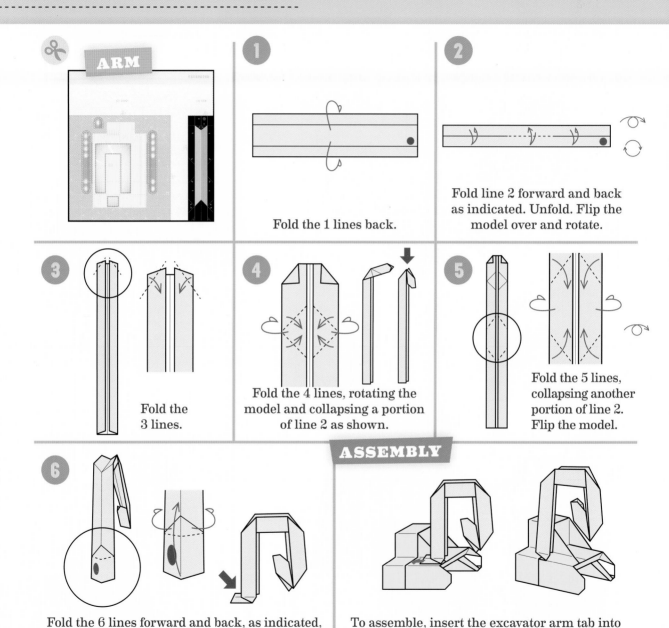

ARM

1 Fold the 1 lines back.

2 Fold line 2 forward and back as indicated. Unfold. Flip the model over and rotate.

3 Fold the 3 lines.

4 Fold the 4 lines, rotating the model and collapsing a portion of line 2 as shown.

5 Fold the 5 lines, collapsing another portion of line 2. Flip the model.

6 Fold the 6 lines forward and back, as indicated, collapsing as shown.

ASSEMBLY

To assemble, insert the excavator arm tab into the pocket on the base as shown.

FRONT-END LOADER

LEVEL ⭐⭐⭐⭐

Cities always have some kind of construction going on. With this front loader, you can break ground and build your city! It has a large bucket on the front to move heavy gravel and dirt and to keep jobsites tidy. Scoop up the rubble, and then dump it into a dump truck (pages 23 and 31) to transport it out of town.

Number of Folding Papers: 2

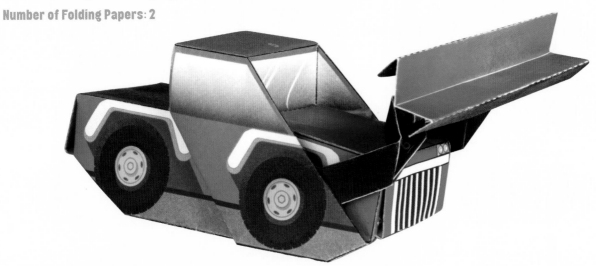

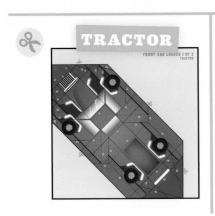

TRACTOR

FRONT-END LOADER 1 OF 2
TRACTOR

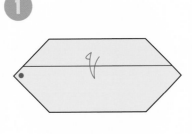

1

Fold line 1 back and unfold.

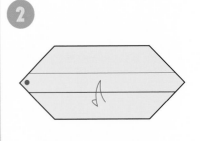

2

Fold line 2 back and unfold.

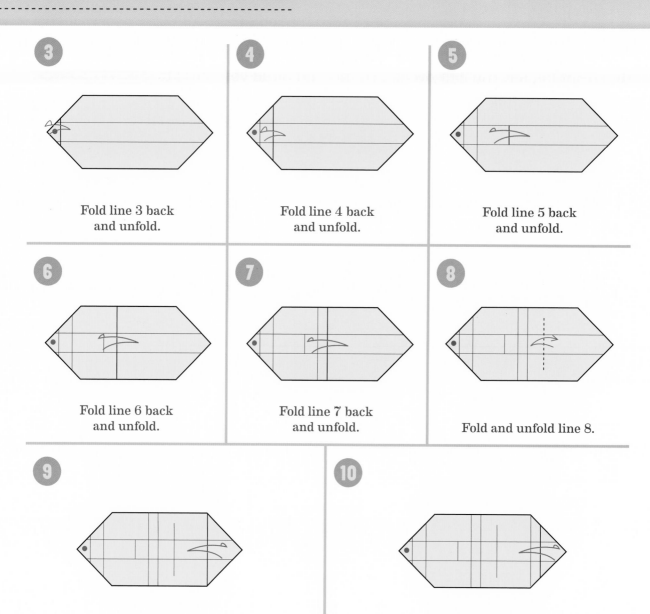

3 Fold line 3 back and unfold.

4 Fold line 4 back and unfold.

5 Fold line 5 back and unfold.

6 Fold line 6 back and unfold.

7 Fold line 7 back and unfold.

8 Fold and unfold line 8.

9 Fold line 9 back and unfold.

10 Fold line 10 back and unfold.

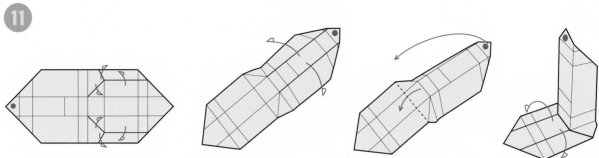

Fold the 11 lines back and refold lines 8, 7, 1, and 2 as shown.

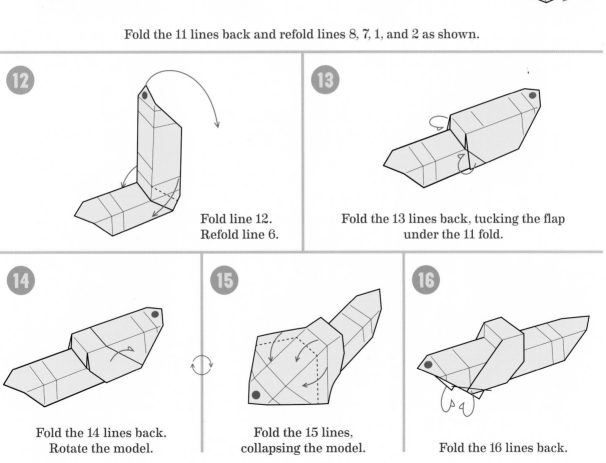

Fold line 12.
Refold line 6.

Fold the 13 lines back, tucking the flap under the 11 fold.

Fold the 14 lines back.
Rotate the model.

Fold the 15 lines,
collapsing the model.

Fold the 16 lines back.

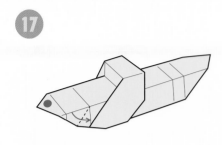

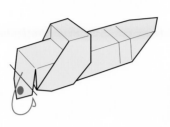

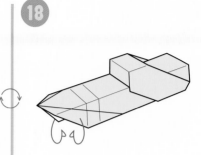

Fold the 17 lines. Refold lines 1, 2 and 4, collapsing the model as shown. Refold line 3, tucking the flap inside and locking the sides. Rotate the model.

Fold the 18 lines back.

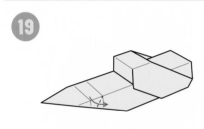

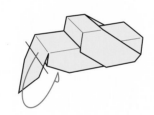

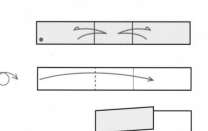

Fold the 19 lines. Refold lines 1, 2, and 9, collapsing the model as shown. Refold line 10, tucking the flap inside and locking the sides. Set the tractor aside.

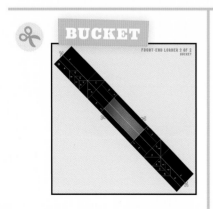

BUCKET

FRONT-END LOADER 2 OF 2
BUCKET

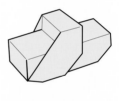

Fold the 1 lines back and unfold. Flip the model over. Refold one of the 1 lines as shown.

2

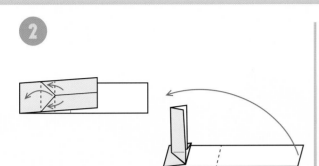

Fold the visible 2 lines. Then refold the second
1 line and repeat the process.

3

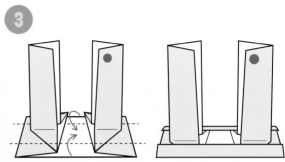

Fold the 3 lines.

4

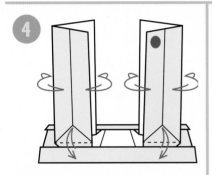

Fold and unfold all the 4 lines.

5

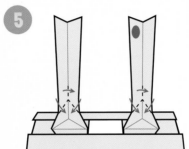

Fold the 5 lines.

6

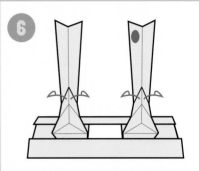

Fold the 6 lines back.

7

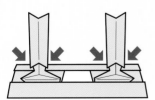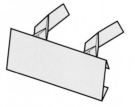

Refold the 4 lines and collapse the model as shown.
Rotate the model.

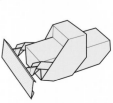

Insert the
arms of the
bucket into
the pockets in
the cab made
by lines 14
and 15.

PLANE LEVEL ★★★★★

This airplane requires four sheets of folding paper and is the most challenging project in this book. But once you complete the plane, your city has wings—find the runway on the mat, start the engines, and take off! And when it's not soaring through the sky, you can park your airplane at the airport (page 96).

Number of Folding Papers: 4

For this project, tile and tape four sheets together to form one large folding paper. Then cut as marked.

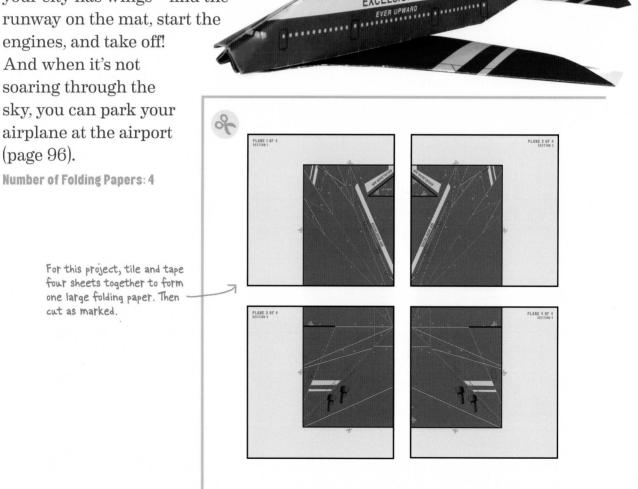

60

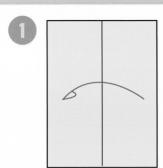

1

Fold line 1 back.

2

Fold and unfold the 2 lines.
Unfold the 1 line.

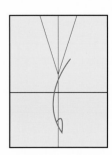

3

Fold the 3 line back.

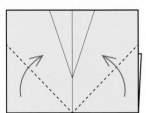

4

Fold the 4 lines.

5

Fold the 5 lines. Completely unfold all the lines
and set the model with the art facing up.

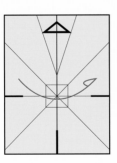

6

Refold line 1
and cut along
the 6 lines.
Unfold
completely.

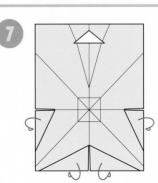

7

Fold the 7 lines back.

61

8

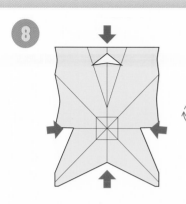

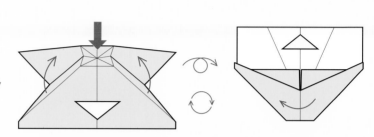

Refold the 3, 4 and 5 lines and collapse as shown. Flip and rotate the model. Refold line 1 along the wing only and move so both wings are on the left side.

9

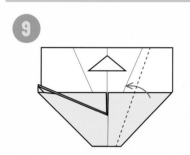

Fold line 9.

10

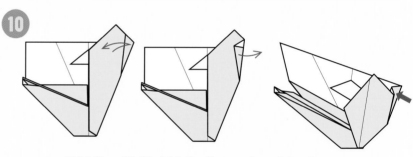

Fold line 10. Unfold the flap and push in the center line so the 10 lines touch.

11

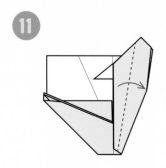

Fold line 11.

12

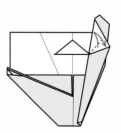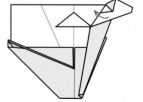

Fold line 12 down and unfold.

 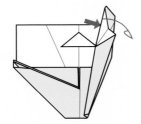 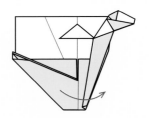

Open slightly to reveal line 13. Fold line 13 and collapse pocket refolding the 12 lines.
Swing the folded wings to the right side and repeat steps 9 through 13 on the left side.

 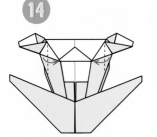 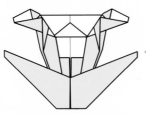

Fold the 14 lines. Flip the model over.

 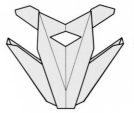

Refold the 2 lines, folding all of the layers
underneath. Pinch so the 2 lines meet and
collapse the model as shown. Rotate the model.

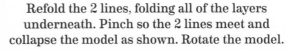

Fold line 16 so wing is up.

Fold line 17 so wing folds down.

Tuck the folded portion
inside the plane. Repeat
on the second wing.

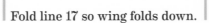

Fold the 19 lines and tuck through the body so that the tail extends upward off the back of the plane.

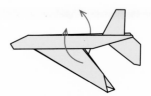

Crease the wings up along the sides of the cabin of the plane.

  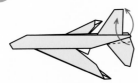

Fold the 21 lines so the tail sections are parallel to the wings.

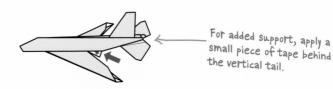

For added support, apply a small piece of tape behind the vertical tail.

Fold the remaining tab of paper protruding from the underside of the plane and tuck inside. If desired, secure the bottom of the plane together with a small piece of clear tape.

HOUSE LEVEL ★★★☆

There are enough folding papers in this kit to fold 6 houses, but the most important one is *your* house! What can you do to make it a home? Will you build it next to an ice cream shop (page 83)? Or how about giving it a big backyard with plenty of space for a pet golden retriever (page 138) to run around?

Number of Folding Papers: 1

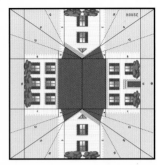

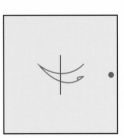

1

Fold line 1 back and unfold.

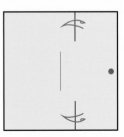

2

Fold the 2 lines back and unfold.

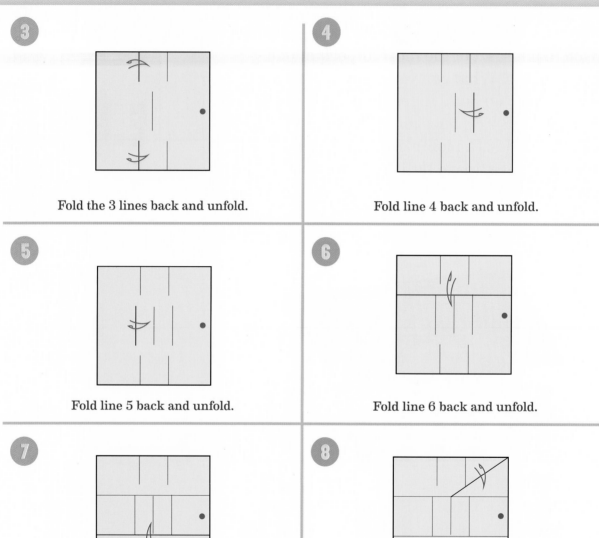

3 Fold the 3 lines back and unfold.

4 Fold line 4 back and unfold.

5 Fold line 5 back and unfold.

6 Fold line 6 back and unfold.

7 Fold line 7 back and unfold.

8 Fold line 8 back and unfold.

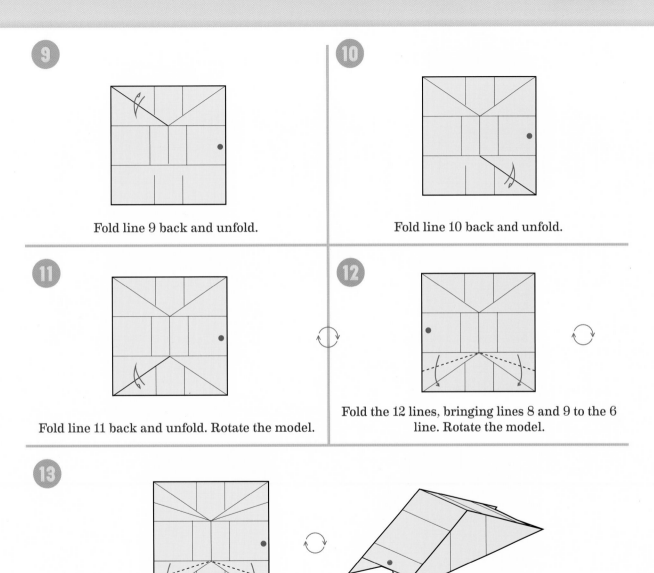

9 Fold line 9 back and unfold.

10 Fold line 10 back and unfold.

11 Fold line 11 back and unfold. Rotate the model.

12 Fold the 12 lines, bringing lines 8 and 9 to the 6 line. Rotate the model.

13 Fold the 13 lines, bringing lines 10 and 11 to the 7 line. Collapse the model and rotate as shown.

67

14

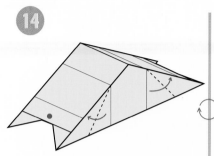

Fold the 14 lines, bringing line 2 to line 8 and line 3 to line 9. Rotate the model.

15

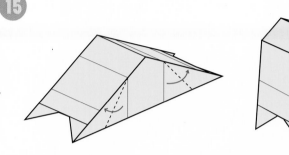

Fold the 15 lines, bringing line 3 to line 11 and line 2 to line 10. Collapse the model as shown.

16

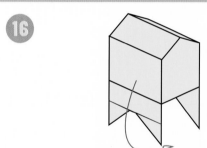

Fold line 16 back, tucking it inside and locking folds 12, 13, 14, and 15 in place. Rotate the model.

17

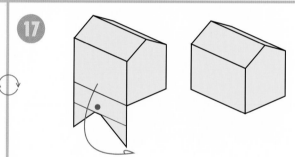

Fold line 17 back, tucking it inside and locking folds 12, 13, 14, and 15 in place. The model is complete.

TOWN HALL LEVEL ★★☆★

This town hall has two large wings with plenty of space for neighbors to come together and spend time with one another. It even has a clock tower that chimes on the hour for the whole city to hear—as long as you provide the sound effects! **Number of Folding Papers: 4**

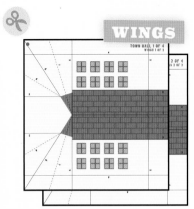

WINGS

TOWN HALL 1 OF 4
WINGS 1 OF 2

2 OF 4
S 2 OF 2

1

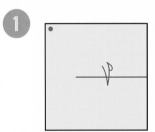

Beginning with one wing of the building, fold line 1 back and unfold.

2

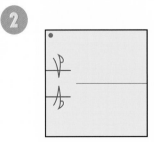

Fold the 2 lines back and unfold.

Fold the 3 lines back
and unfold.

Fold the 4 lines back
and unfold.

Fold the 5 lines back.
Unfold one 5 line as shown.

Fold the 6 lines
back and unfold.

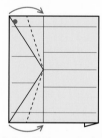

Fold the 7 lines, bringing
the 5 and 6 lines together,
collapsing the model.

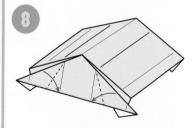

Fold the 8 lines, bringing the
2 and 6 lines together,
collapsing the model.

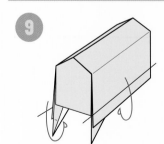

Refold the 4 lines, tucking the
flaps inside and locking folds
1, 2, 5, 6, and 8 in place.

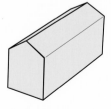

Set aside the first wing and
repeat steps 1 through 9 on the
second wing of the building.

CENTER STRUCTURE

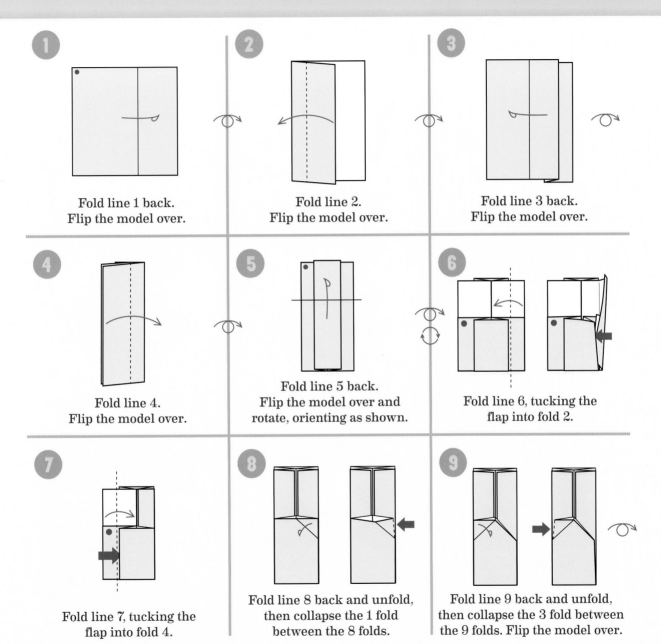

1 Fold line 1 back.
Flip the model over.

2 Fold line 2.
Flip the model over.

3 Fold line 3 back.
Flip the model over.

4 Fold line 4.
Flip the model over.

5 Fold line 5 back.
Flip the model over and
rotate, orienting as shown.

6 Fold line 6, tucking the
flap into fold 2.

7 Fold line 7, tucking the
flap into fold 4.

8 Fold line 8 back and unfold,
then collapse the 1 fold
between the 8 folds.

9 Fold line 9 back and unfold,
then collapse the 3 fold between
the 9 folds. Flip the model over.

Fold line 10 and unfold slightly.

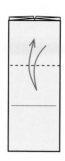

Fold line 11 and unfold slightly.
Flip the center structure over and set it aside.

CLOCK TOWER

TOWN HALL 4 OF 4
CLOCK TOWER

Fold line 1 in front and unfold.

Fold the 2 line back and unfold.

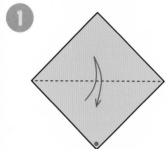

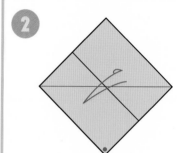

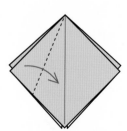

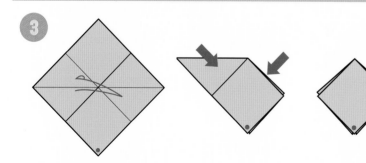

Fold the 3 line back and unfold. Then refold lines 2 and 3,
collapsing the 1 folds together.

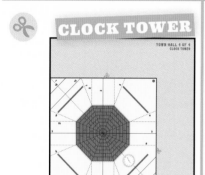

Fold line 4.

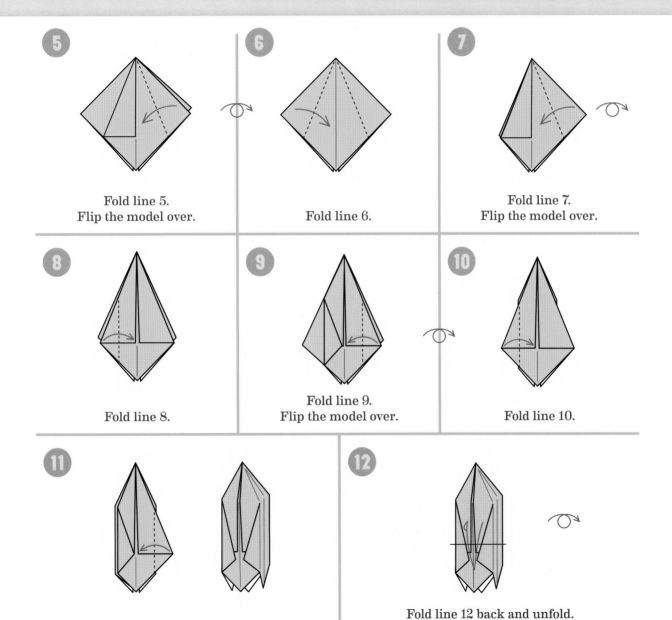

5

Fold line 5.
Flip the model over.

6

Fold line 6.

7

Fold line 7.
Flip the model over.

8

Fold line 8.

9

Fold line 9.
Flip the model over.

10

Fold line 10.

11

Fold line 11.

12

Fold line 12 back and unfold.
Flip the model over.

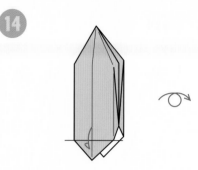

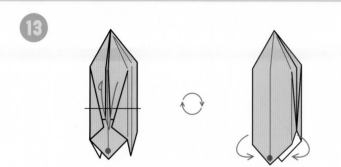

13 Fold line 13 back and unfold. Rotate the model and tuck in the flaps created by folds 12 and 13.

14 Fold line 14 back. Flip the model over.

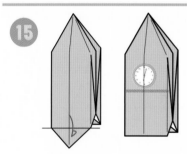

15 Fold line 15 back. Set aside clock tower.

1 Connect the wings by sliding the 5 folds into the 2 and 4 folds of the center structure as shown.

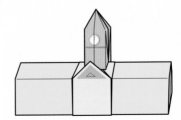

2 Place the clock tower on top of the center structure.

SCHOOL LEVEL ★★☆☆

Every city needs a school, so kids have a place to learn and play! Complete the school yard with a swing set in the back (page 124), or a bus lane where school buses (page 2) line up and drop off kids before the morning bell. Maybe you can organize a field trip to learn about the chipmunks and rabbits (pages 145 and 147) that live in the nearby park!

Number of Folding Papers: 3

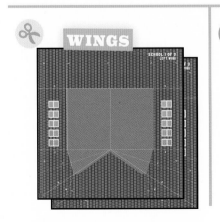

Beginning with one wing of the building, fold line 1 back and unfold.

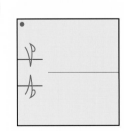

Fold the 2 lines back and unfold.

Fold the 3 lines back
and unfold.

Fold the 4 lines back
and unfold.

Fold the 5 lines back.
Unfold one 5 line as shown.

Fold the 6 lines
back and unfold.

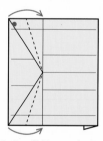

Fold the 7 lines, bringing
the 5 and 6 lines together,
collapsing the model.

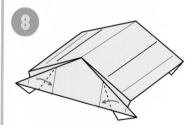

Fold the 8 lines, bringing the
2 and 6 lines together,
collapsing the model.

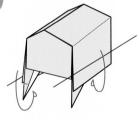

Refold the 4 lines, tucking the
flaps inside and locking folds
1, 2, 5, 6, and 8 in place.

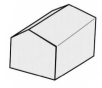

Set aside the first wing and
repeat steps 1 through 9 on the
second wing of the building.

CENTER STRUCTURE

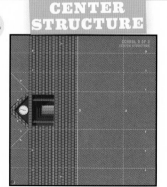

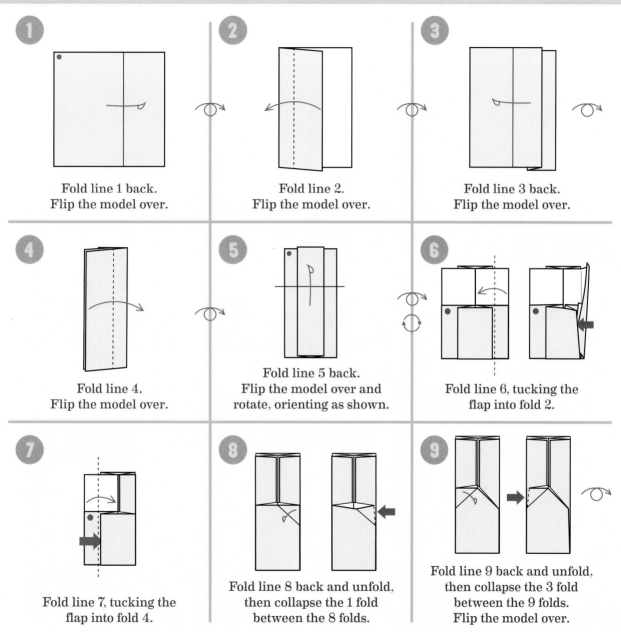

1 Fold line 1 back.
Flip the model over.

2 Fold line 2.
Flip the model over.

3 Fold line 3 back.
Flip the model over.

4 Fold line 4.
Flip the model over.

5 Fold line 5 back.
Flip the model over and
rotate, orienting as shown.

6 Fold line 6, tucking the
flap into fold 2.

7 Fold line 7, tucking the
flap into fold 4.

8 Fold line 8 back and unfold,
then collapse the 1 fold
between the 8 folds.

9 Fold line 9 back and unfold,
then collapse the 3 fold
between the 9 folds.
Flip the model over.

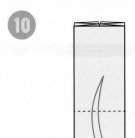

10

Fold line 10 and unfold slightly.

11

Fold line 11 and unfold slightly.
Flip the center structure over and set it aside.

ASSEMBLY

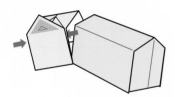 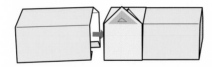 

Connect the wings by sliding the 5 folds into the
2 and 4 folds of the center structure as shown.

FIRE STATION LEVEL ★★☆☆

Fire stations and the firefighters who work in them are an important part of every city. They help save people from fires and other dangerous accidents. This fire station has an open door so you can park the hook and ladder truck (page 46) or the pumper truck (page 21) inside. Plus, complete your fire station with a resident Dalmatian (page 138)!

Number of Folding Papers: 2

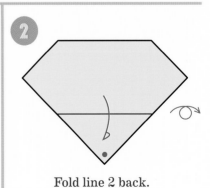

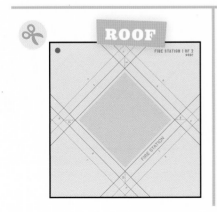

ROOF

FIRE STATION 1 OF 2

FIRE STATION

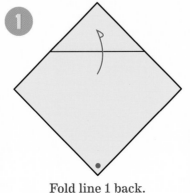

1

Fold line 1 back.

2

Fold line 2 back.
Flip the model over.

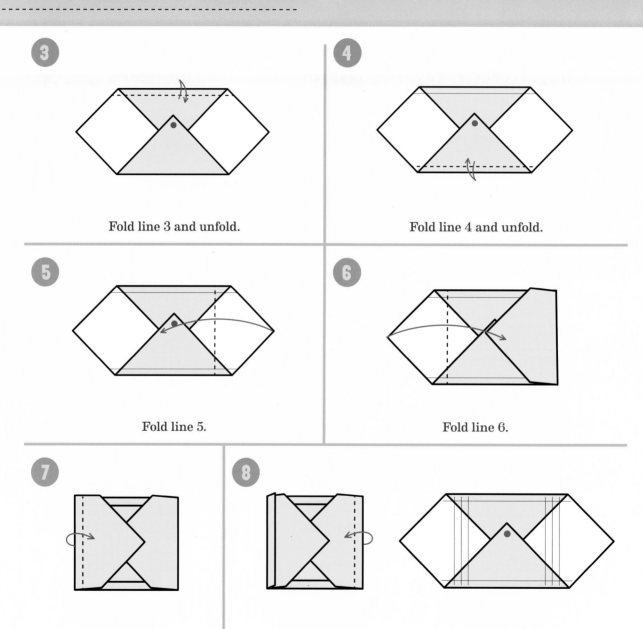

3 Fold line 3 and unfold.

4 Fold line 4 and unfold.

5 Fold line 5.

6 Fold line 6.

7 Fold line 7.

8 Fold line 8. Then unfold lines 8, 7, 6, and 5.

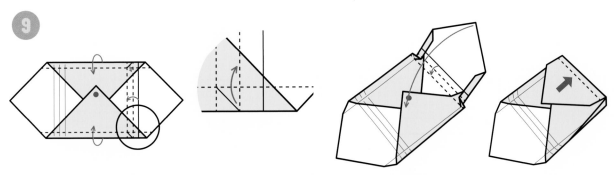

Fold the 9 lines, collapsing the model, as shown. Refold line 5 and crease line 8 on its fold, tucking and locking the two corners.

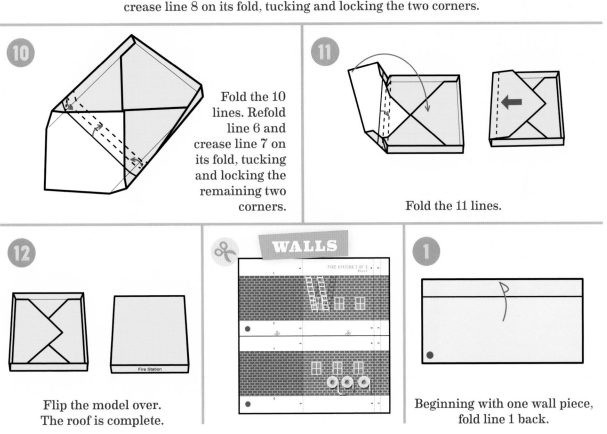

Fold the 10 lines. Refold line 6 and crease line 7 on its fold, tucking and locking the remaining two corners.

Fold the 11 lines.

Flip the model over. The roof is complete.

Beginning with one wall piece, fold line 1 back.

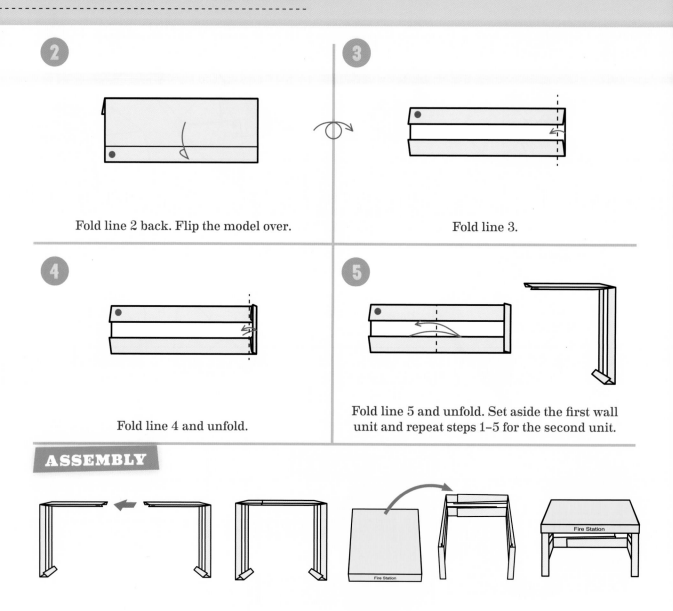

2

Fold line 2 back. Flip the model over.

3

Fold line 3.

4

Fold line 4 and unfold.

5

Fold line 5 and unfold. Set aside the first wall unit and repeat steps 1–5 for the second unit.

ASSEMBLY

Fire Station

Fire Station

Attach the two wall units by sliding the tabs with the red dots together. Slide the tabs almost all the way in so that the back of the station is about one wall wide. Place the roof on top of the walls.

ICE CREAM SHOP LEVEL ★☆☆☆

There are so many great places to build an ice cream shop. Where is best for your city? It could be in the park (page 127), where hungry kids will be ready for a treat. You could even build it right next door to *your* house!

Number of Folding Papers: 2

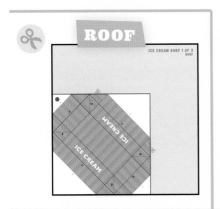

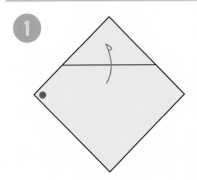

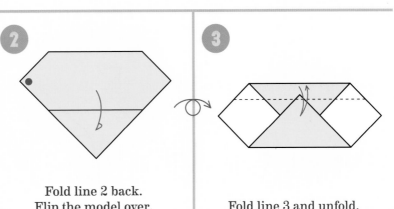

1

Fold line 1 back.

2

Fold line 2 back.
Flip the model over.

3

Fold line 3 and unfold.

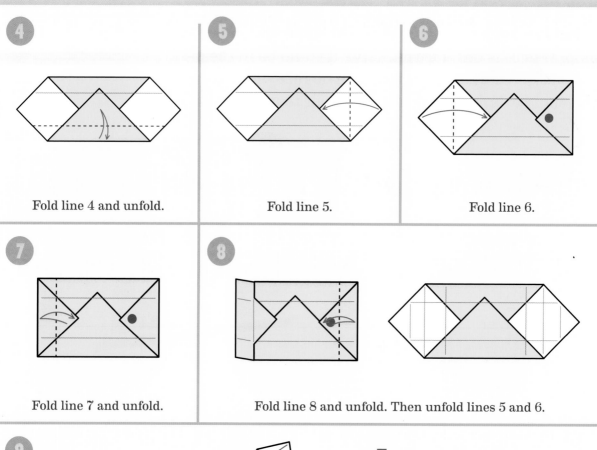

Fold line 4 and unfold.

Fold line 5.

Fold line 6.

Fold line 7 and unfold.

Fold line 8 and unfold. Then unfold lines 5 and 6.

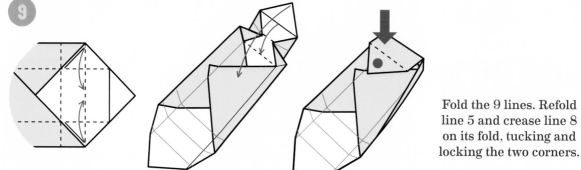

Fold the 9 lines. Refold line 5 and crease line 8 on its fold, tucking and locking the two corners.

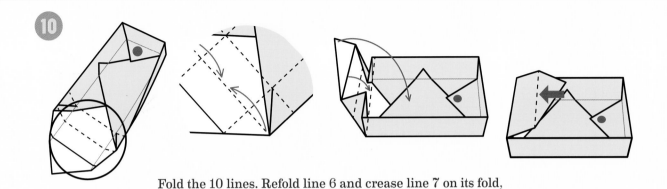

Fold the 10 lines. Refold line 6 and crease line 7 on its fold, tucking and locking the two remaining corners.

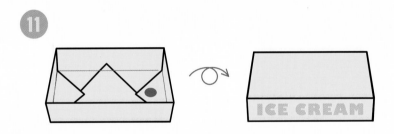

Flip the model over. The roof is complete.

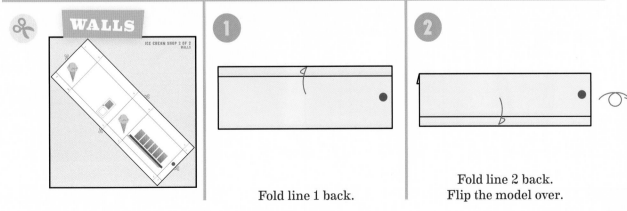

WALLS

ICE CREAM SHOP 2 OF 2
WALLS

Fold line 1 back.

Fold line 2 back.
Flip the model over.

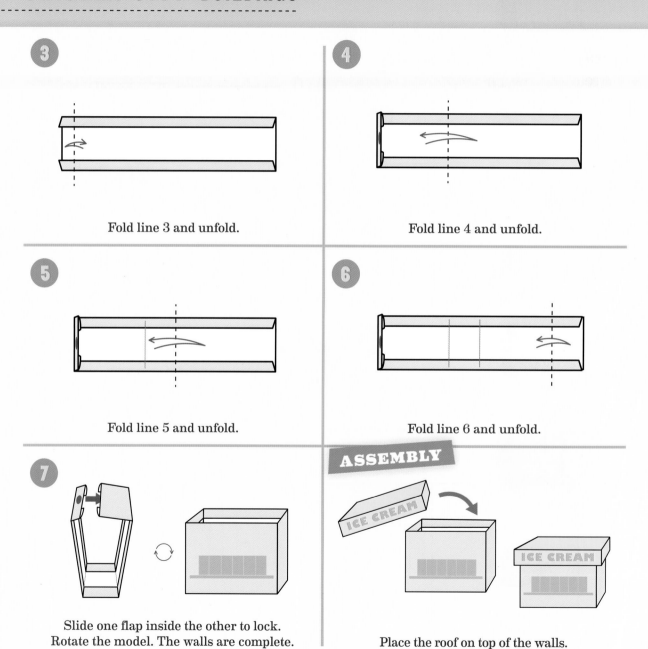

3

Fold line 3 and unfold.

4

Fold line 4 and unfold.

5

Fold line 5 and unfold.

6

Fold line 6 and unfold.

7

Slide one flap inside the other to lock.
Rotate the model. The walls are complete.

ASSEMBLY

ICE CREAM

ICE CREAM

Place the roof on top of the walls.

LIBRARY LEVEL ★☆★★

Local libraries have lots of character and are a great place for communities to gather. What makes the library in your city special? Does it have a resident cat (page 143) that roams the aisles? Or maybe it's primely located next to the ice cream shop (page 83)!

Number of Folding Papers: 3

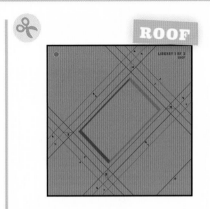

ROOF

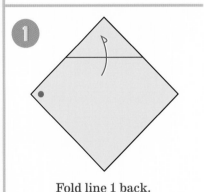

1

Fold line 1 back.

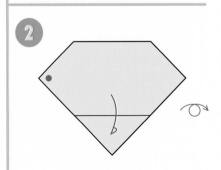

2

Fold line 2 back.
Flip the model over.

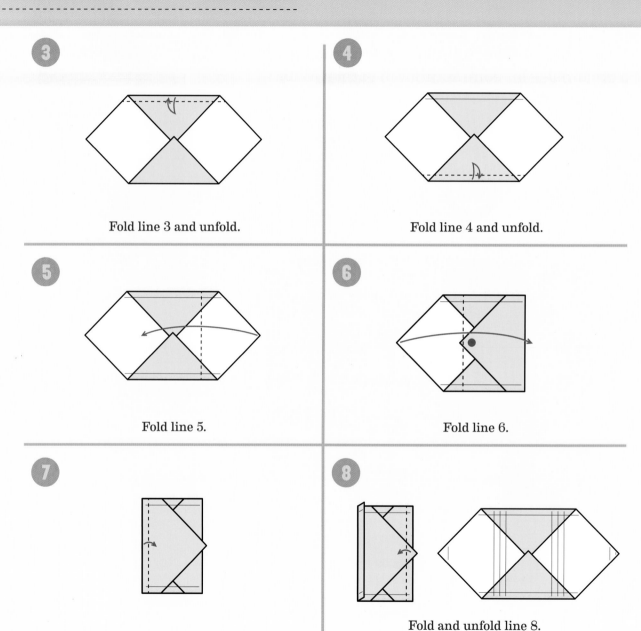

Fold line 3 and unfold.

Fold line 4 and unfold.

Fold line 5.

Fold line 6.

Fold line 7.

Fold and unfold line 8.
Then unfold lines 7, 6, and 5.

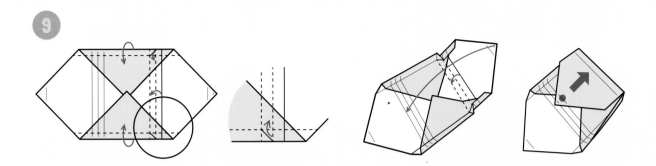

Fold the 9 lines. Refold line 5 and crease line 8 on its fold, tucking and locking the two corners.

Fold the 10 lines. Refold line 6 and crease line 7 on its fold, tucking and locking the remaining two corners.

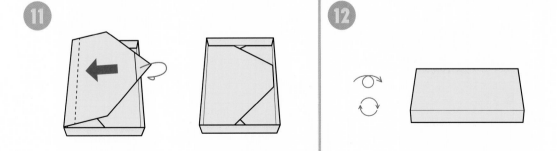

Fold the 11 line back to tuck the corner.

Flip the model over. The roof is complete.

ORIGAMI CITY: BUILDINGS

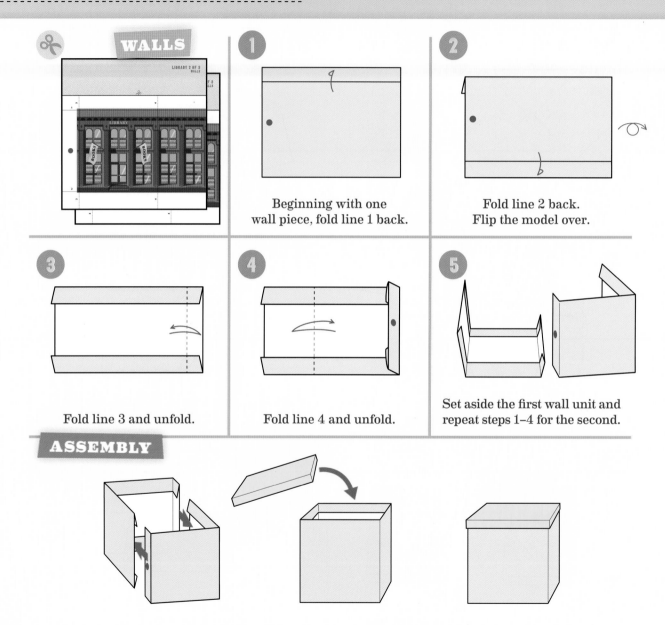

WALLS

LIBRARY 2 OF 3
WALLS

1
Beginning with one
wall piece, fold line 1 back.

2
Fold line 2 back.
Flip the model over.

3
Fold line 3 and unfold.

4
Fold line 4 and unfold.

5
Set aside the first wall unit and
repeat steps 1–4 for the second.

ASSEMBLY

Attach the two wall units by sliding the tabs together. Place the roof on top of the walls.

APARTMENT BUILDING LEVEL ★★★★

Apartment buildings come in all sizes and are home to many families. Some are so tall they scrape the sky, while others have just a few floors. How many stories will your building have?

Number of Folding Papers: 5

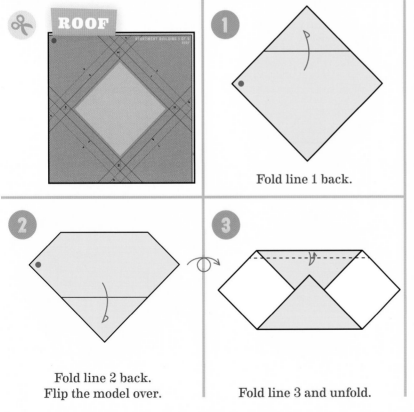

✂ **ROOF**

1

Fold line 1 back.

2

Fold line 2 back.
Flip the model over.

3

Fold line 3 and unfold.

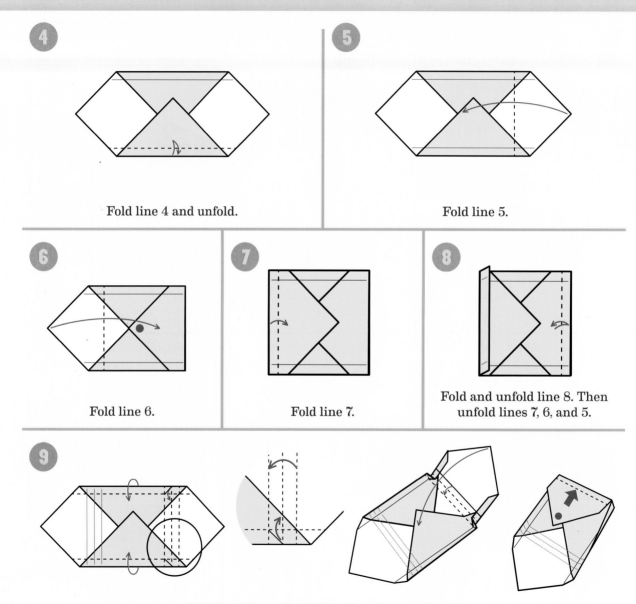

4 Fold line 4 and unfold.

5 Fold line 5.

6 Fold line 6.

7 Fold line 7.

8 Fold and unfold line 8. Then unfold lines 7, 6, and 5.

9 Fold the 9 lines. Refold line 5 and crease line 8 on its fold, tucking and locking the two corners.

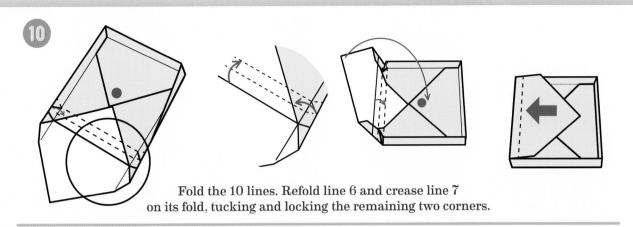

Fold the 10 lines. Refold line 6 and crease line 7
on its fold, tucking and locking the remaining two corners.

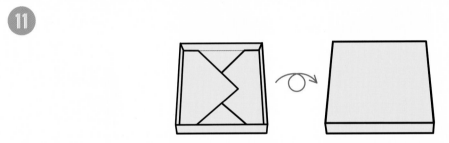

Flip the model over. The roof is complete.

TOP WALLS

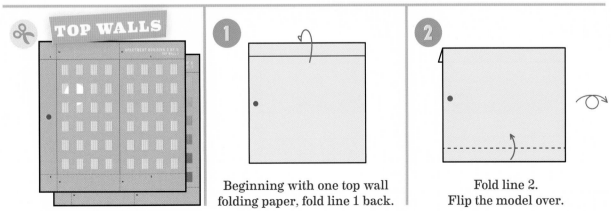

Beginning with one top wall
folding paper, fold line 1 back.

Fold line 2.
Flip the model over.

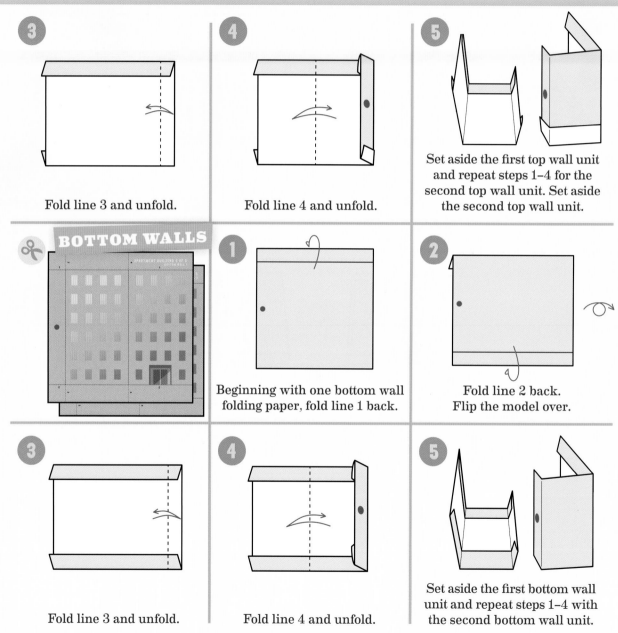

3 Fold line 3 and unfold.

4 Fold line 4 and unfold.

5 Set aside the first top wall unit and repeat steps 1–4 for the second top wall unit. Set aside the second top wall unit.

BOTTOM WALLS

1 Beginning with one bottom wall folding paper, fold line 1 back.

2 Fold line 2 back. Flip the model over.

3 Fold line 3 and unfold.

4 Fold line 4 and unfold.

5 Set aside the first bottom wall unit and repeat steps 1–4 with the second bottom wall unit.

ASSEMBLY

1

Attach the first top wall unit and the first bottom wall unit by inserting fold 2 of the top into fold 1 of the bottom.

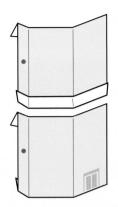
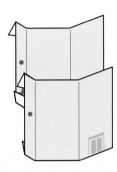

2

Repeat step 1 to attach the second top and second bottom wall units.

3

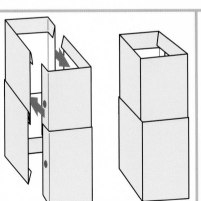

Attach the two wall units by sliding the tabs together.

4

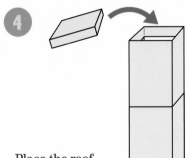

Place the roof on top of the walls.

AIRPORT LEVEL ★☆★★

With so many people coming and going, airports are a hub of activity. You will need lots of space to park the airplane (page 60), so build somewhere with lots of open space. And don't forget to line your runway with traffic cones (page 130) and airport blockades (page 131) for safe takeoff! **Number of Folding Papers: 3**

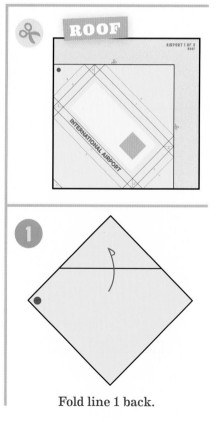

✂ ROOF

AIRPORT 1 OF 3
ROOF

INTERNATIONAL AIRPORT

1

Fold line 1 back.

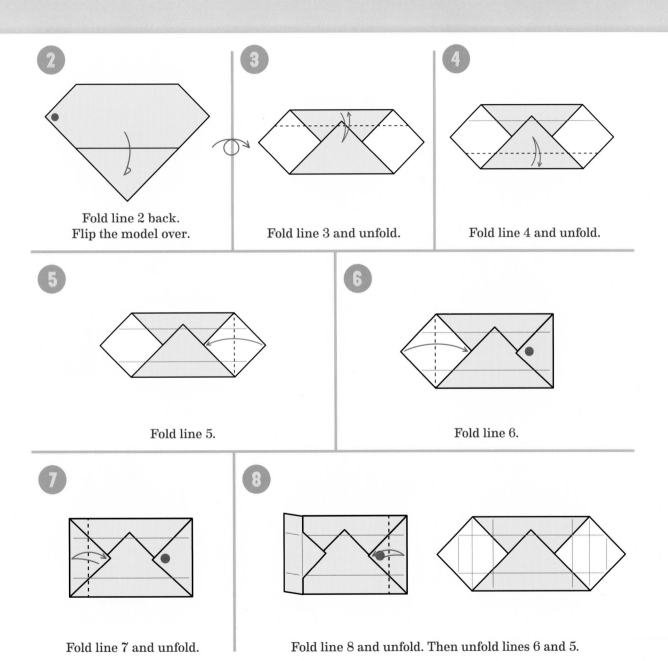

2 Fold line 2 back.
Flip the model over.

3 Fold line 3 and unfold.

4 Fold line 4 and unfold.

5 Fold line 5.

6 Fold line 6.

7 Fold line 7 and unfold.

8 Fold line 8 and unfold. Then unfold lines 6 and 5.

97

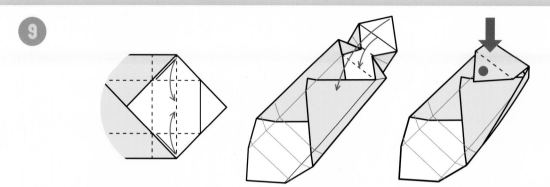

Fold the 9 lines. Refold line 5 and crease line 8 on its fold, tucking and locking the two corners.

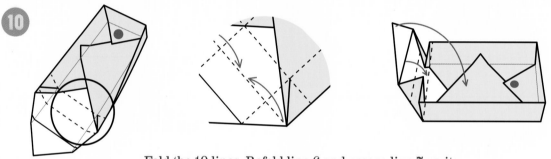

Fold the 10 lines. Refold line 6 and crease line 7 on its fold, tucking and locking the remaining two corners.

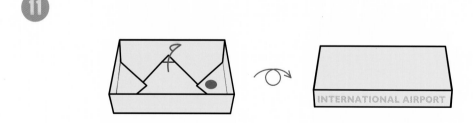

Fold 11 line back to tuck in the corner. Flip the model over. The roof is complete.

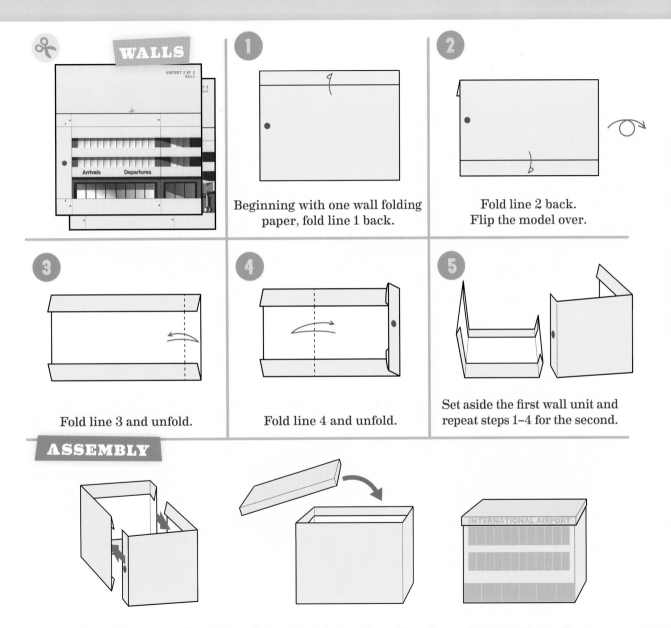

WALLS

1 Beginning with one wall folding paper, fold line 1 back.

2 Fold line 2 back. Flip the model over.

3 Fold line 3 and unfold.

4 Fold line 4 and unfold.

5 Set aside the first wall unit and repeat steps 1–4 for the second.

ASSEMBLY

Attach the two wall units by sliding the tabs together. Place the roof on top of the walls.

HOSPITAL LEVEL ★✩★★

Build a hospital so the people in your city have a place to see a doctor. Make sure you place it somewhere with plenty of space for ambulances (page 4) and other rescue vehicles to arrive and drop off patients, and for cars (page 13) to park when friends and family come to visit.

Number of Folding Papers: 3

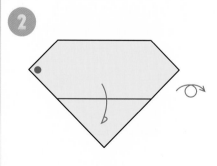

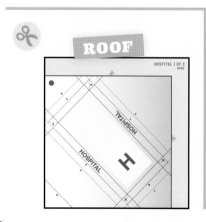

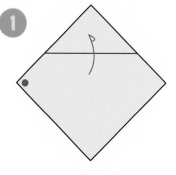

Fold line 1 back.

Fold line 2 back.
Flip the model over.

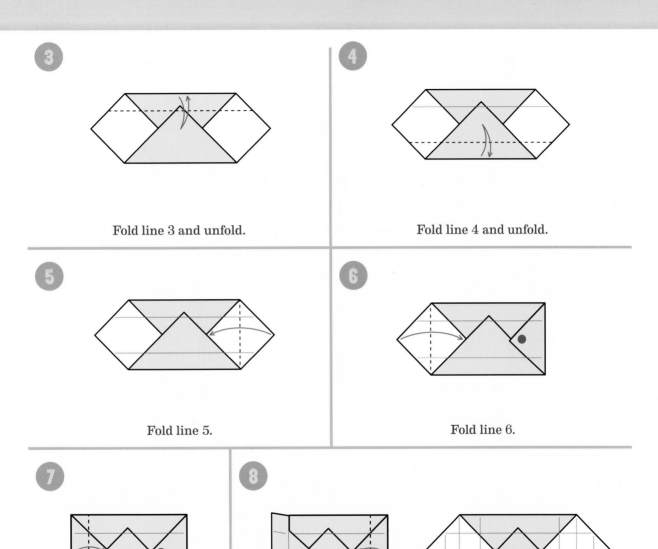

3

Fold line 3 and unfold.

4

Fold line 4 and unfold.

5

Fold line 5.

6

Fold line 6.

7

Fold line 7 and unfold.

8

Fold line 8 and unfold. Then unfold lines 6 and 5.

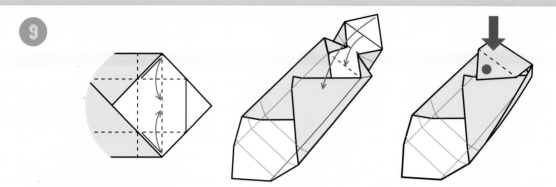

Fold the 9 lines. Refold line 5 and crease line 8 on its fold, tucking and locking the two corners.

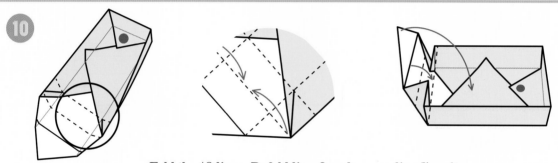

Fold the 10 lines. Refold line 6 and crease line 7 on its fold, tucking and locking the remaining two corners.

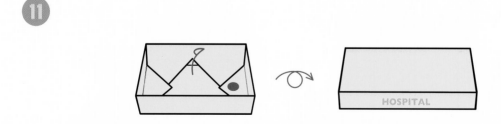

Fold 11 line back to tuck in the corner. Flip the model over. The roof is complete.

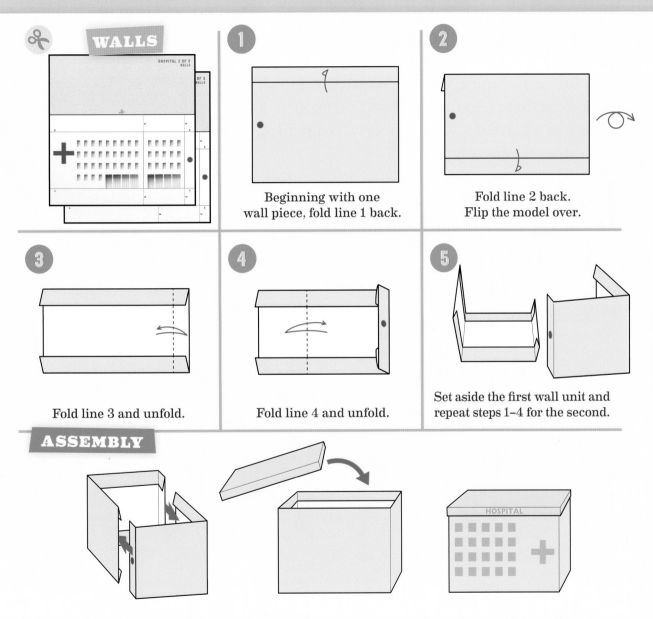

WALLS

HOSPITAL 2 OF 3
WALLS

OF 3
WALLS

1

Beginning with one
wall piece, fold line 1 back.

2

Fold line 2 back.
Flip the model over.

3

Fold line 3 and unfold.

4

Fold line 4 and unfold.

5

Set aside the first wall unit and
repeat steps 1–4 for the second.

ASSEMBLY

HOSPITAL

Attach the two wall units by sliding the tabs together. Place the roof on top of the walls.

103

POLICE STATION

LEVEL ★★★★

Every city has a police station so police officers have a place to work and meet with people from the community. What makes your station special? Is there a fountain (page 128) right outside or a garden with lots of trees (page 132)?

Number of Folding Papers: 3

ROOF

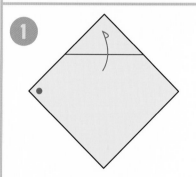

1

Fold line 1 back.

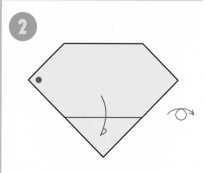

2

Fold line 2 back.
Flip the model over.

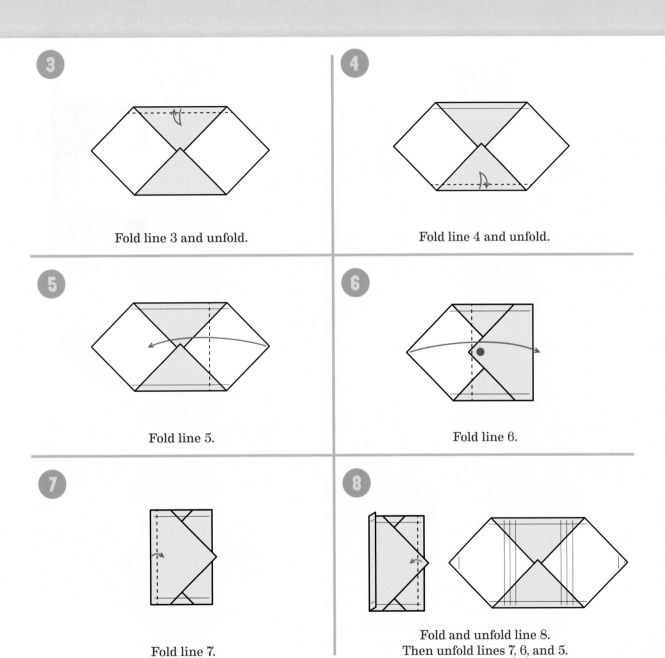

3 Fold line 3 and unfold.

4 Fold line 4 and unfold.

5 Fold line 5.

6 Fold line 6.

7 Fold line 7.

8 Fold and unfold line 8.
Then unfold lines 7, 6, and 5.

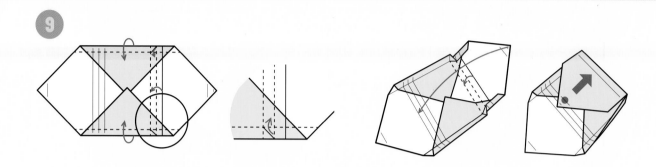

Fold the 9 lines. Refold line 5 and crease line 8 on its fold, tucking and locking the two corners.

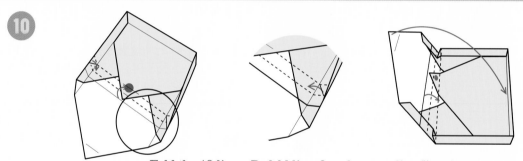

Fold the 10 lines. Refold line 6 and crease line 7 on its fold, tucking and locking the remaining two corners.

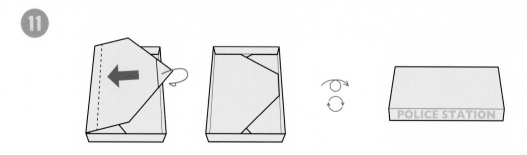

Fold the 11 line back to tuck the corner. Flip the model over. The roof is complete.

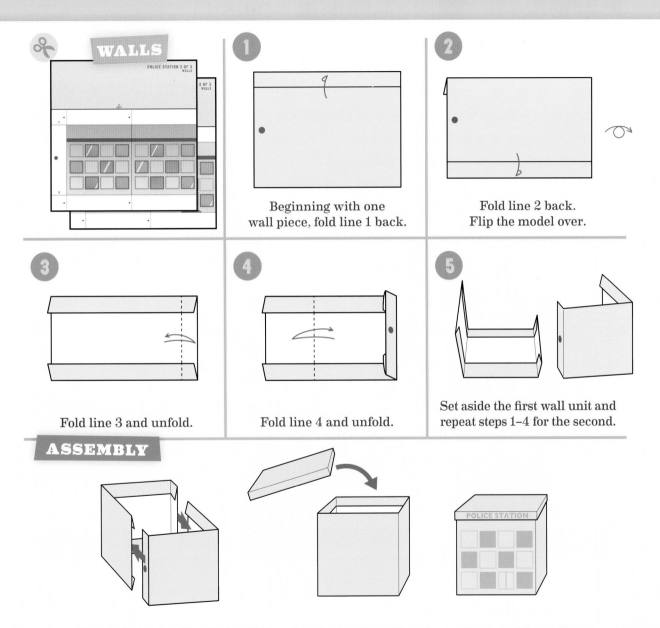

WALLS

POLICE STATION 2 OF 3
WALLS

3 OF 3
WALLS

1 Beginning with one wall piece, fold line 1 back.

2 Fold line 2 back. Flip the model over.

3 Fold line 3 and unfold.

4 Fold line 4 and unfold.

5 Set aside the first wall unit and repeat steps 1–4 for the second.

ASSEMBLY

POLICE STATION

Attach the two wall units by sliding the tabs together. Place the roof on top of the walls.

107

PUBLIC MAILBOX LEVEL ★★⯪☆

Public mailboxes are peppered across cities so people can send mail anytime, anyplace. Where will you put mailboxes in your city? On Main Street where there are lots of shops? Or maybe outside an apartment building (page 91) where lots of people live. This folding sheet has two mailboxes so once you get the folds down, you can make another one! **Number of Folding Papers: 1**

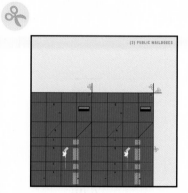

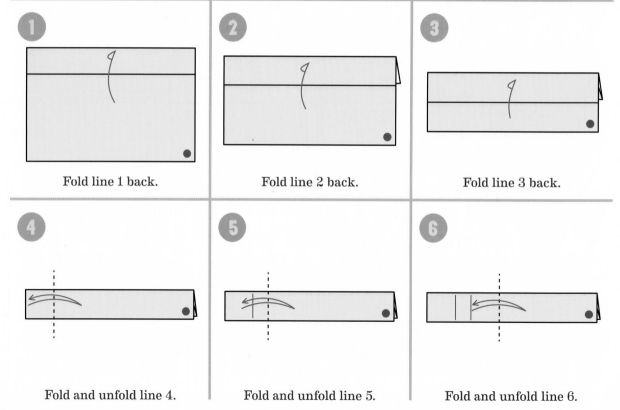

1

Fold line 1 back.

2

Fold line 2 back.

3

Fold line 3 back.

4

Fold and unfold line 4.

5

Fold and unfold line 5.

6

Fold and unfold line 6.

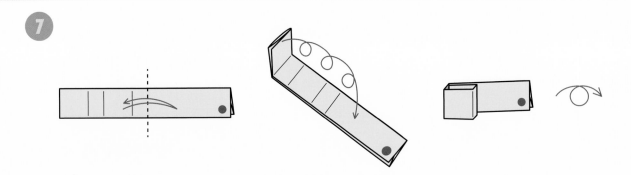

7

Fold and unfold line 7, then refold lines 4, 5, 6, and 7, gently "rolling" the model. Flip the model over.

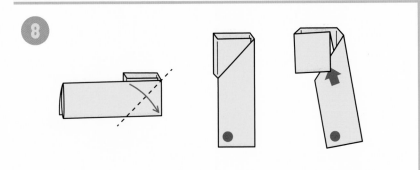

8

Fold line 8. Tuck the crease made by fold 8 inside fold 2.

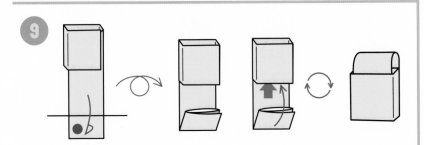

9

Fold line 9 back. Flip the model over. Tuck the flap inside the box as shown. Rotate the model so it stands on its own.

PERSONAL MAILBOX LEVEL ★★★★

Personal mailboxes are where postal workers deliver mail addressed to a specific home address. So when you fold a house (page 65), make sure you fold a personal mailbox to go with it. **Number of Folding Papers: 1**

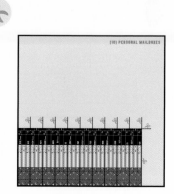

(10) PERSONAL MAILBOXES

1

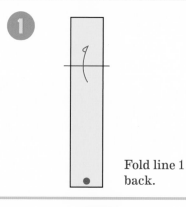

Fold line 1 back.

2

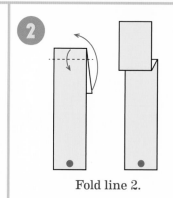

Fold line 2.

3

Fold line 3 back.

4

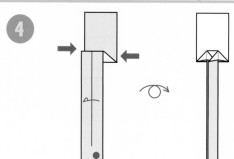

Fold the 4 line back. Flip the model over and collapse the corners, as shown.

5

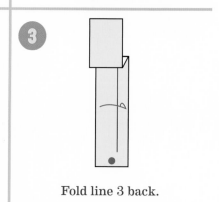

Unfold lines 3 and 4 near the base. Fold line 5 back, collapsing the corners as shown. Flip the model over.

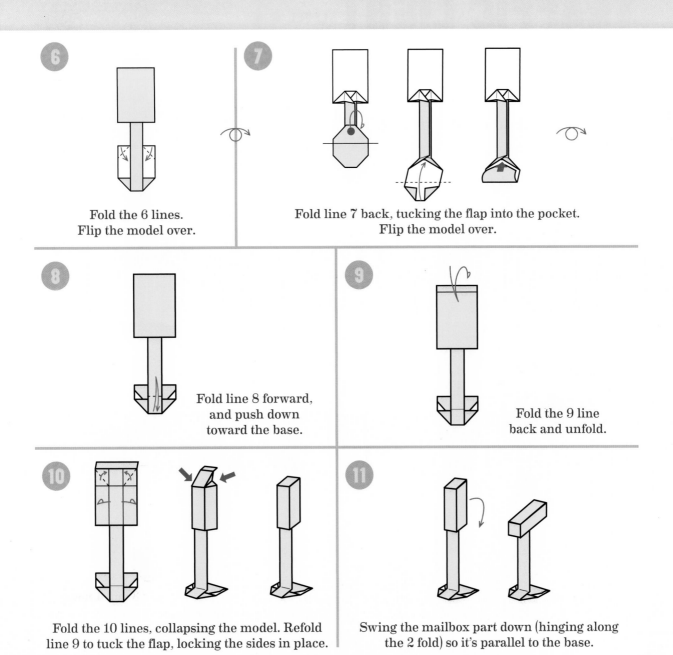

6 Fold the 6 lines.
Flip the model over.

7 Fold line 7 back, tucking the flap into the pocket.
Flip the model over.

8 Fold line 8 forward,
and push down
toward the base.

9 Fold the 9 line
back and unfold.

10 Fold the 10 lines, collapsing the model. Refold
line 9 to tuck the flap, locking the sides in place.

11 Swing the mailbox part down (hinging along
the 2 fold) so it's parallel to the base.

111

TRAFFIC LIGHT LEVEL ★★★★

Traffic lights keep people safe in any city. Everyone knows: Green means go, yellow means slow down, and red means STOP! Place them at busy intersections in your city to keep traffic moving smoothly! **Number of Folding Papers: 1**

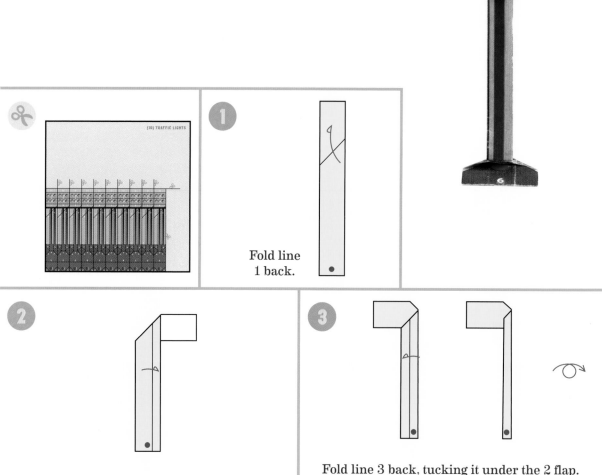

1 Fold line 1 back.

2 Fold line 2 back.

3 Fold line 3 back, tucking it under the 2 flap. Flip the model over.

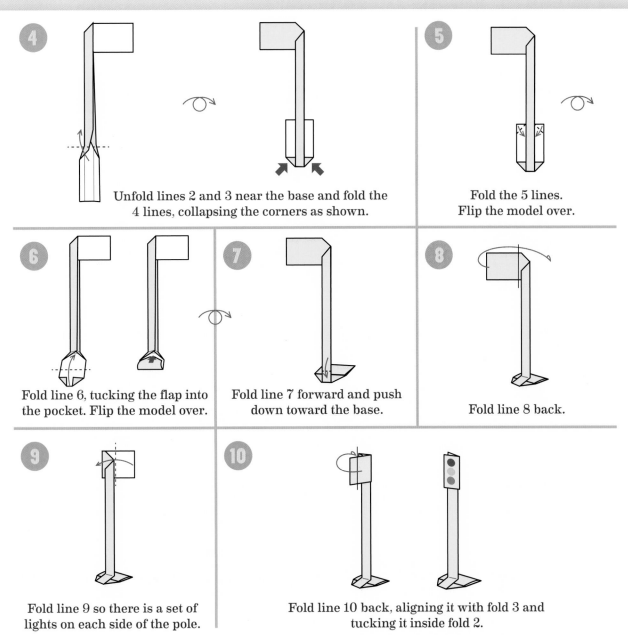

4 Unfold lines 2 and 3 near the base and fold the 4 lines, collapsing the corners as shown.

5 Fold the 5 lines. Flip the model over.

6 Fold line 6, tucking the flap into the pocket. Flip the model over.

7 Fold line 7 forward and push down toward the base.

8 Fold line 8 back.

9 Fold line 9 so there is a set of lights on each side of the pole.

10 Fold line 10 back, aligning it with fold 3 and tucking it inside fold 2.

TRAFFIC SIGNS LEVEL ★½★★

Traffic signs tell drivers and pedestrians when to stop for other cars, where to watch out for icy patches of road, where to park, and much more. What do the drivers in your city need to look out for? Is there a pesky pothole that never gets filled (slow down!) or a family of ducks that lives in the park and likes to cross the road? **Number of Folding Papers: 1**

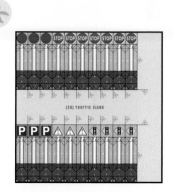

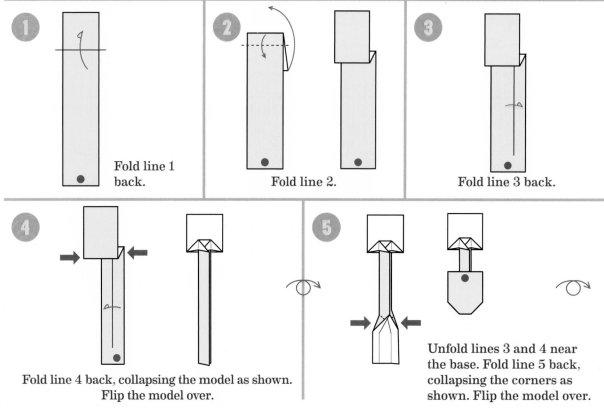

1 Fold line 1 back.

2 Fold line 2.

3 Fold line 3 back.

4 Fold line 4 back, collapsing the model as shown. Flip the model over.

5 Unfold lines 3 and 4 near the base. Fold line 5 back, collapsing the corners as shown. Flip the model over.

114

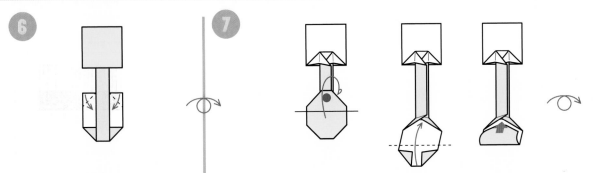

6 Fold the 6 lines.
Flip the model over.

7 Fold line 7 back, tucking the flap into the pocket.
Flip the model over.

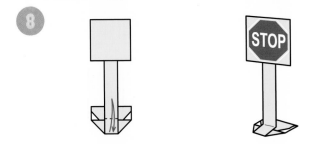

8 Fold line 8 forward and push
down toward the base.

STREETLAMP

Streetlamps keep city streets well lit at night so that drivers and pedestrians can see where they are going, and stay safe. Where will you place the streetlamps in your city? **Number of Folding Papers: 1**

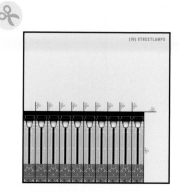

1 Fold line 1 back.

2 Fold line 2.

3 Fold line 3 back.

4 Fold line 4 back, collapsing the model as shown. Flip the model over.

5 Unfold lines 3 and 4 near the base and fold the 5 lines, collapsing the corners as shown. Flip the model over.

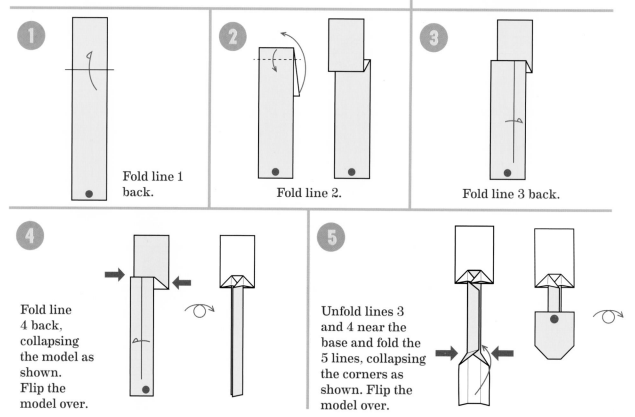

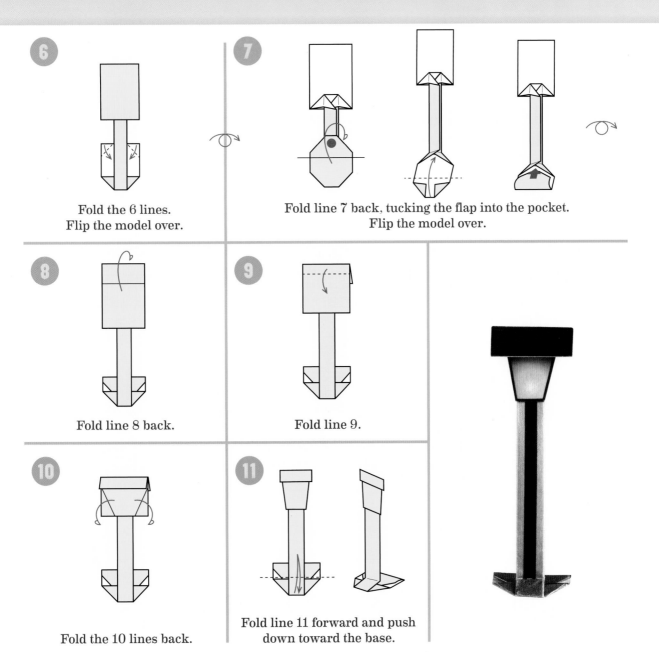

6 Fold the 6 lines.
Flip the model over.

7 Fold line 7 back, tucking the flap into the pocket.
Flip the model over.

8 Fold line 8 back.

9 Fold line 9.

10 Fold the 10 lines back.

11 Fold line 11 forward and push
down toward the base.

117

FLAGS LEVEL ★★★

You'll notice there are two flags on this folding paper. One represents the United States of America, and one represents Japan. Japan is where author and origami expert Taro Yaguchi is from, and it is often considered to be the birthplace of origami. There are even a few blank flags for you to decorate yourself—fly them proudly in your city! **Number of Folding Papers: 1**

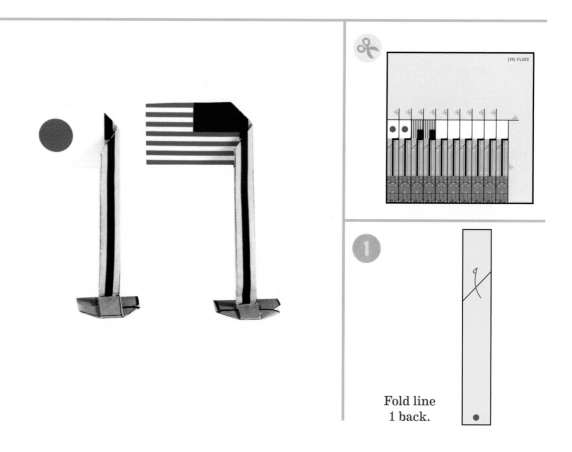

Fold line
1 back.

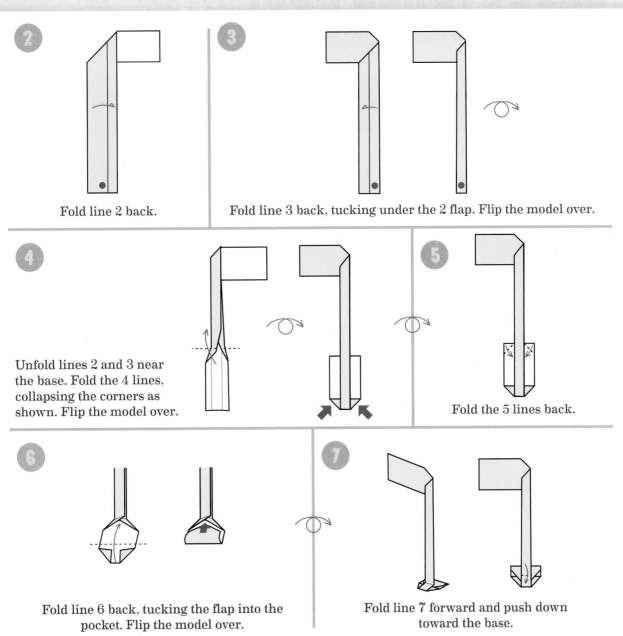

2 Fold line 2 back.

3 Fold line 3 back, tucking under the 2 flap. Flip the model over.

4 Unfold lines 2 and 3 near the base. Fold the 4 lines, collapsing the corners as shown. Flip the model over.

5 Fold the 5 lines back.

6 Fold line 6 back, tucking the flap into the pocket. Flip the model over.

7 Fold line 7 forward and push down toward the base.

BASKETBALL HOOP LEVEL ★★⯪★

You'll notice that the traffic signs, the flags, and the streetlamp all share the same basic folds. Once you've learned them, you're halfway done with the basketball hoop. Fold a couple and set up a court at the playground. Then crumple a scrap of paper into a ball and practice your slam dunk! **Number of Folding Papers: 1**

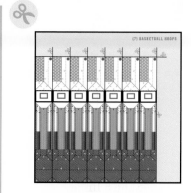

1

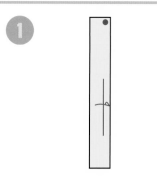

Fold line 1 back and unfold.

2

Fold line 2 back and unfold.

3

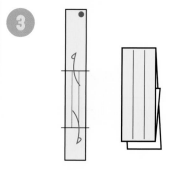

Fold the 3 lines back.

4

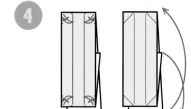

Fold and unfold the 4 lines. Completely unfold the model.

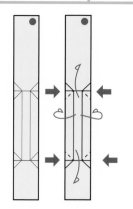

Refold lines 1 and 2, folding the two pole flaps over each other and collapsing the 3 and 4 folds as shown.

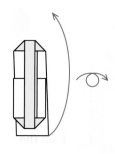

Lift the back flap slightly and flip the model over.

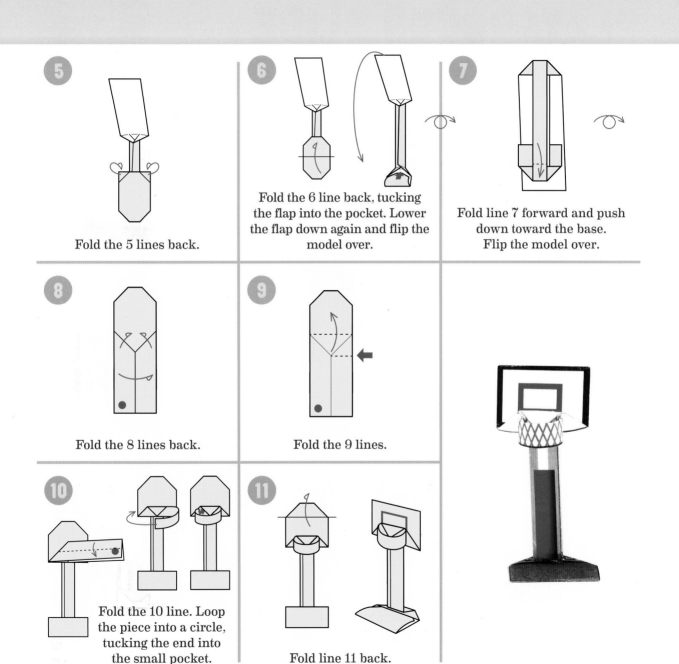

5 Fold the 5 lines back.

6 Fold the 6 line back, tucking the flap into the pocket. Lower the flap down again and flip the model over.

7 Fold line 7 forward and push down toward the base. Flip the model over.

8 Fold the 8 lines back.

9 Fold the 9 lines.

10 Fold the 10 line. Loop the piece into a circle, tucking the end into the small pocket.

11 Fold line 11 back.

PLAYGROUND SLIDE LEVEL ★★★★

Slides are a playground must-have—a thrilling time from the tip-top of the ladder to sliding into the wood chips or sand at the bottom. You could even mix things up and make it a waterslide by setting it up to end with a splash in the fountain (page 128)!

Number of Folding Papers: 1

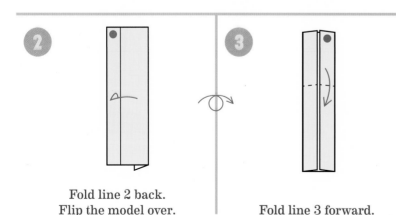

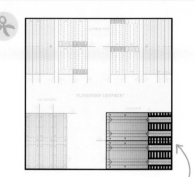

There are multiple projects on this folding paper. Cut out the playground slide.

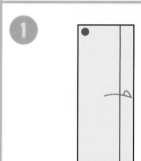

1

Fold line 1 back.

2

Fold line 2 back.
Flip the model over.

3

Fold line 3 forward.

4

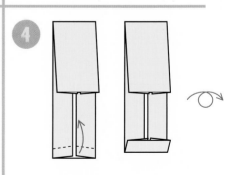

Fold line 4.
Flip the model over.

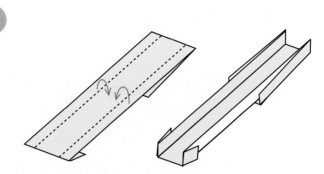

Fold the 5 lines forward.

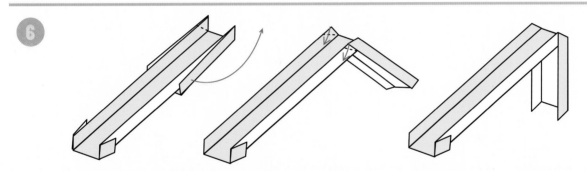

Partially unfold line 3 in order to fold the 6 lines.

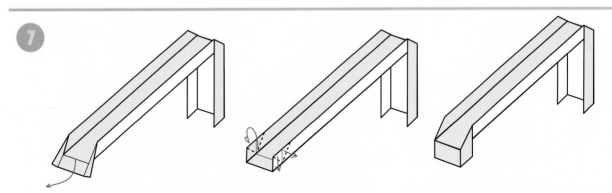

Partially unfold line 4 in order to fold the 7 lines.

PLAYGROUND SWING SET LEVEL ⭐⯪☆☆

What is more fun than hearing the air whistle past your ears as you swing on a swing set? After you've folded and assembled the pieces, you might want to place this colorful swing set on some grass to give kids a soft landing pad.

Number of Folding Papers: 1

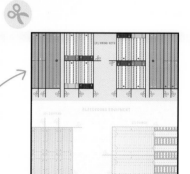

There are multiple projects on this folding paper. Cut out the playground swing set. You should have 4 colored seats, 2 green sides, and 1 purple bar.

SEATS

1

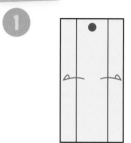

Beginning with one seat piece, fold the 1 lines back.

2

Fold line 2 and let it partially unfold.

3

Set the first seat aside and repeat steps 1 and 2 on the other three seats.

SIDES

1

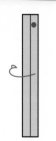

Beginning with one side piece, fold line 1 back.

2

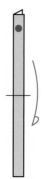

Fold line 2 back.

3

Set the first side piece aside and repeat steps 1 and 2 on the other side piece. Rotate the second folded piece so the open sides face each other. Set them both aside.

124

 1

 1

Fold line 1 back.

 **2**

Fold and unfold line 2.

 **1**

Unfold line 2 on the purple bar.

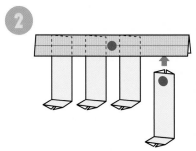 **2**

Insert the top of the seats into fold 1 on the cross bar.

 3

Refold line 2 on the cross bar, locking the seats into place.

 4

Insert the folded ends of the cross bar into fold 2 of each of the sides as shown.

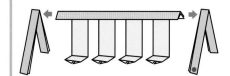

 5

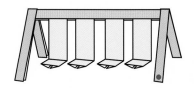

The model is complete and can stand on its own.

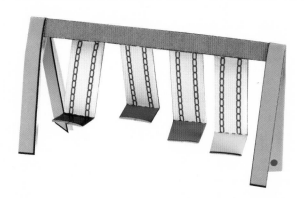

PLAYGROUND SEESAW LEVEL ★★★★

The seesaw is a classic playground activity!
You could put yours at the park (page 127),
by the school (page 75), or even—lucky
you—in your own backyard (page 65)!

Number of Folding Papers: 1

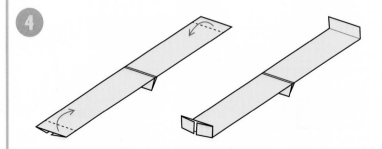

✂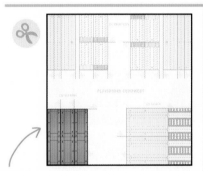

There are multiple projects on this folding
paper. Cut out the playground seesaw.

1

Fold the 1 lines back.

2

Fold line 2.

3

Fold and unfold one 3 line.
Flip the model and repeat.

4

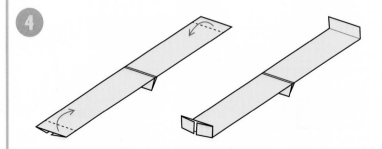

Pinch the 3 lines together and open the ends as shown.
Fold and partially unfold the 4 lines.

PARK BENCH LEVEL ★☆☆☆

What's better than relaxing on a park bench? Pretty much nothing! This bench is easy to fold and will be great to add to the playground so parents can sit while the kids play. There are multiple benches printed on this folding sheet, so you can put benches all over your city! **Number of Folding Papers: 1**

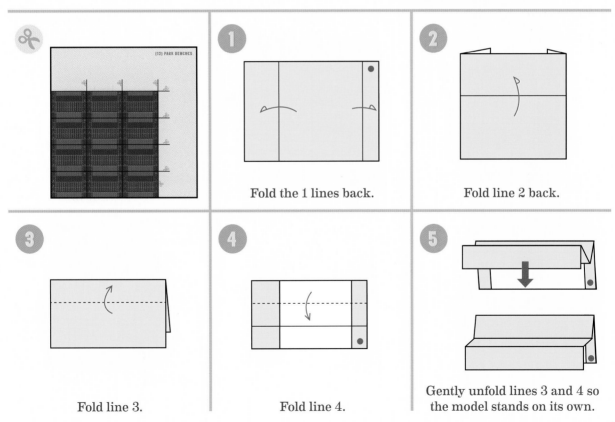

(12) PARK BENCHES	**1** Fold the 1 lines back.	**2** Fold line 2 back.
3 Fold line 3.	**4** Fold line 4.	**5** Gently unfold lines 3 and 4 so the model stands on its own.

FOUNTAIN LEVEL ★★½☆

Grab your scissors! The fountain is one of the rare origami projects that you will cut and fold, in order to form the delicate patterns of cascading water.

Number of Folding Papers: 1

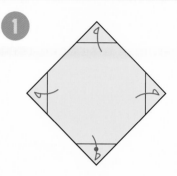

The fountain has 3 pieces. Cut them out before you fold!

1

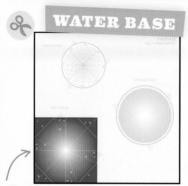

Fold the 1 lines back.

2

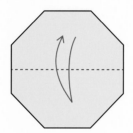

Fold and unfold line 2.

3

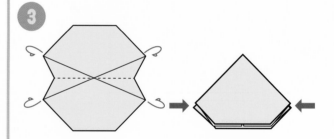

Fold and unfold the 3 lines, then collapse as shown.

4

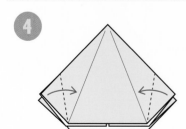

Fold the 4 lines. Flip the model over and fold the remaining 4 lines.

5

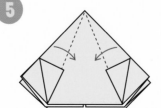

Fold the 5 lines. Flip the model over and fold the remaining 5 lines.

6

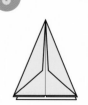

Gently open from the bottom so the model stands on its own.

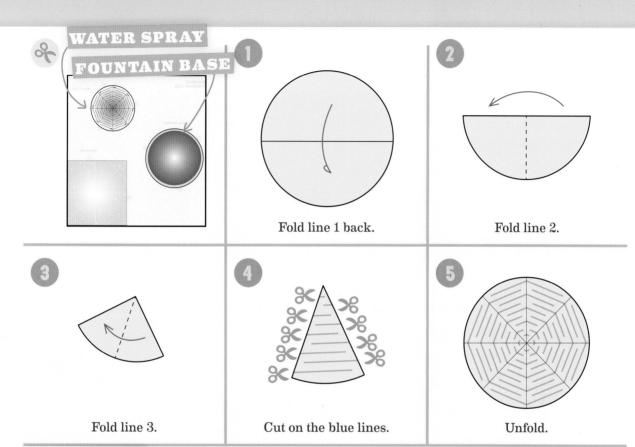

WATER SPRAY FOUNTAIN BASE

1 Fold line 1 back.

2 Fold line 2.

3 Fold line 3.

4 Cut on the blue lines.

5 Unfold.

ASSEMBLY

Place the water base on the fountain base. Balance the water spray on top of the water base.

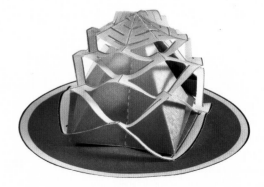

TRAFFIC CONE LEVEL ★★★★

Traffic cones help mark spots on the road where it's dangerous to drive, and construction workers use them to line the areas where they are working. Set up traffic cones by the tanker truck (page 25) or the front-end loader (page 55) to help them get the job done! **Number of Folding Papers: 1**

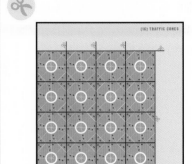

1

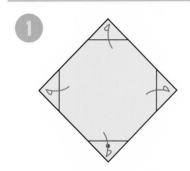

Fold the 1 lines back.

2

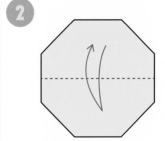

Fold and unfold line 2.

3

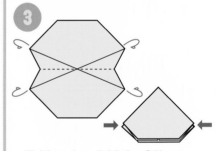

Fold and unfold the 3 lines, then collapse as shown.

4

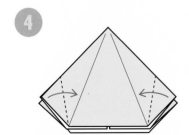

Fold the 4 lines. Flip the model over and fold the remaining 4 lines.

5

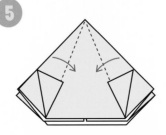

Fold the 5 lines. Flip the model over and fold the remaining 5 lines.

6

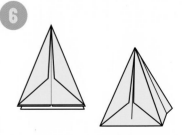

Gently open from the bottom so the model stands on its own.

AIRPORT BLOCKADE  LEVEL ★★★★

Airport blockades are used to keep people, vehicles, and planes from using the same areas at the same time. Carefully place them at the airport to keep everyone safe and traffic moving smoothly. **Number of Folding Papers: 1**

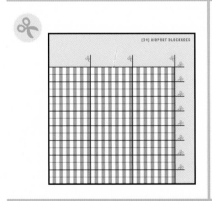

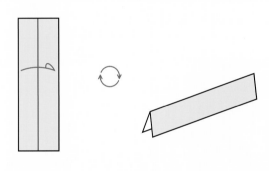

Fold line 1. Rotate the model so it stands on its own.

DECIDUOUS TREE LEVEL ★★★★

Cities need a lot of trees. They're calming and good for the environment. Plus, they make good homes for birds, squirrels, and chipmunks (page 145). You can choose two different color folding sheets to make springtime or autumn foliage. **Number of Folding Papers: 3**

TREE TOP

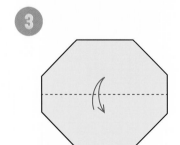

DECIDUOUS TREE 1 OF 3
AUTUMN TREE TOP

1

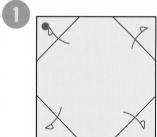

Fold the 1 lines back.

2

Fold the 2 lines back.

3

Fold and unfold line 3.

4

Fold the 4 lines back and unfold. Refold 3 and 4 lines and collapse as shown.

5

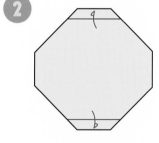

Fold one 5 line forward and one 5 line back, tucking the flaps inside. Set aside tree top.

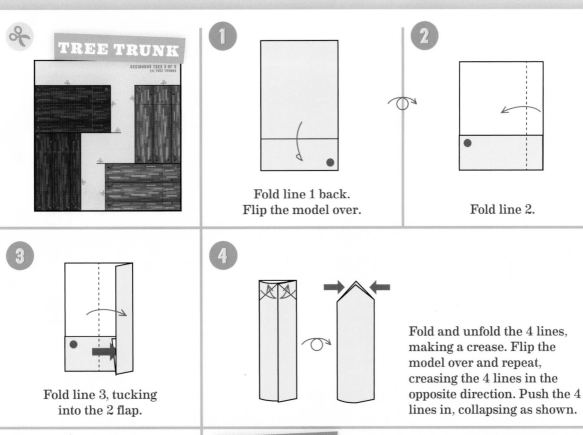

TREE TRUNK

DECIDUOUS TREE 3 OF 3
(4) TREE TRUNKS

1 Fold line 1 back.
Flip the model over.

2 Fold line 2.

3 Fold line 3, tucking into the 2 flap.

4 Fold and unfold the 4 lines, making a crease. Flip the model over and repeat, creasing the 4 lines in the opposite direction. Push the 4 lines in, collapsing as shown.

5 Open up the 2 and 3 tabs at the bottom (leave the top tucked) for stability.

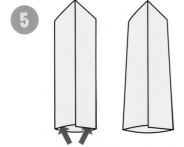

ASSEMBLY

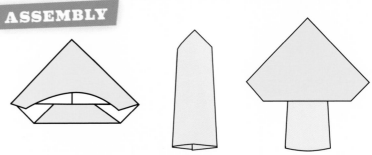

Insert the top of the tree trunk into the bottom of the tree top, resting the 5 folds inside the crevice created by the 4 folds.

133

EVERGREEN TREE

Evergreen trees keep their leaves (called needles) year-round. Some evergreens actually do have green needles, but others have a blue tint to them. What color will you fold first? **Number of Folding Papers: 1**

EVERGREEN TREE 1 OF 2

EVERGREEN TREE 2 OF 2

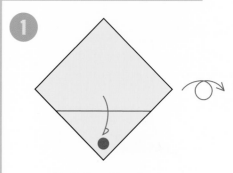

1

Fold line 1 back.
Flip the model over.

134

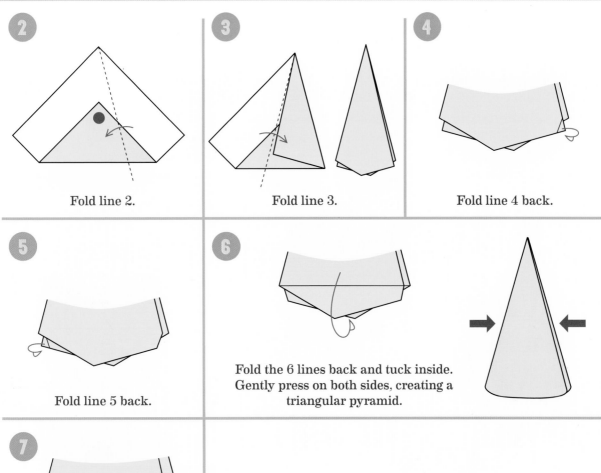

2 Fold line 2.

3 Fold line 3.

4 Fold line 4 back.

5 Fold line 5 back.

6 Fold the 6 lines back and tuck inside. Gently press on both sides, creating a triangular pyramid.

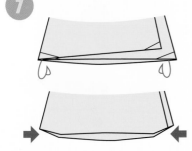

7 Fold the 7 lines back.

BUSH LEVEL ★★★★★

In towns and cities, bushes are sometimes planted as fences to divide a yard from the sidewalk or from other yards. They are also the perfect spot for rabbits (page 147) to burrow and build their nests! **Number of Folding Papers: 1**

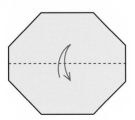

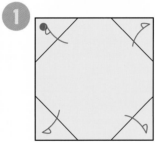

Fold the 1 lines back.

Fold the 2 lines back.

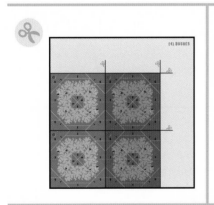

Fold and unfold line 3.

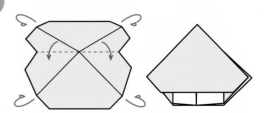

Fold the 4 lines back and unfold. Refold the 3 and 4 lines, collapsing as shown.

5

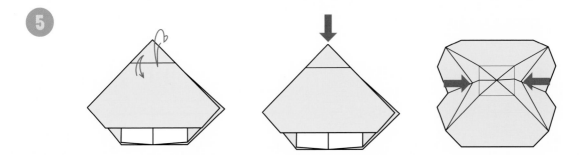

Fold the 5 line forward and back. Partially unfold and gently
press on the top point to collapse as shown.

6

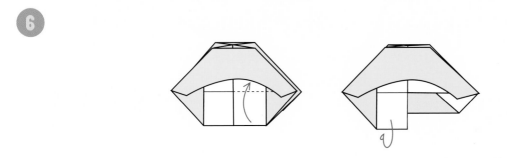

Fold one 6 line forward and one 6 line back, tucking the flaps inside.

7

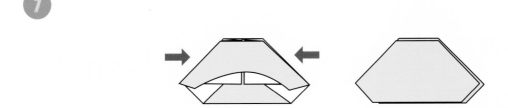

Puff out the bush by gently pushing the sides in for added stability.

DOG LEVEL ★★★★

They say dogs are a human's best friend. City dwellers definitely agree—they are known to bring their dogs everywhere! To the grocery store, the library (page 87), even in taxis (page 13)! Where is the most unexpected place you've seen someone bring a dog? **Number of Folding Papers: 1**

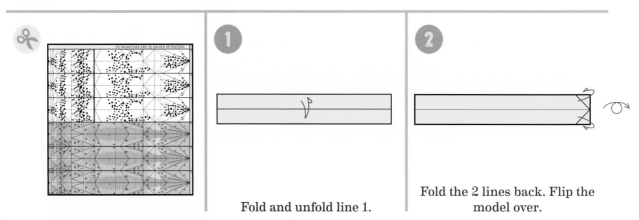

1

Fold and unfold line 1.

2

Fold the 2 lines back. Flip the model over.

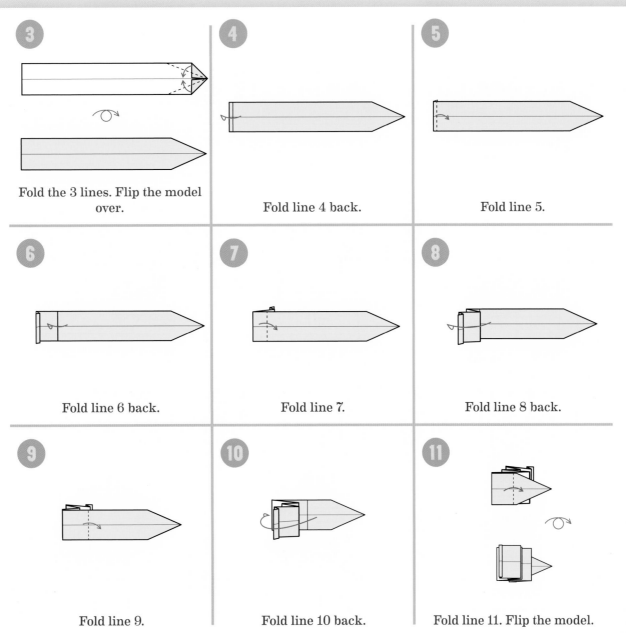

3 Fold the 3 lines. Flip the model over.

4 Fold line 4 back.

5 Fold line 5.

6 Fold line 6 back.

7 Fold line 7.

8 Fold line 8 back.

9 Fold line 9.

10 Fold line 10 back.

11 Fold line 11. Flip the model.

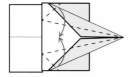 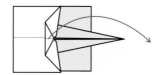 

Fold the 12 lines, collapsing as shown. Unfold line 10. Flip the model over.

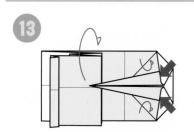

Fold the 13 lines and refold the 1 line, collapsing the tail section inward.

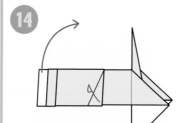

Unfold slightly to fold the 14 lines back.

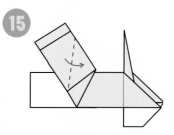

Unfold slightly to fold the 15 lines forward.

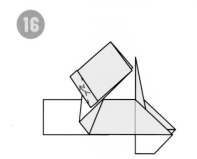

Fold the 16 lines.

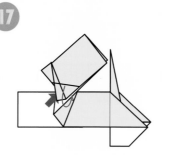

Fold the 17 lines back, tucking the flap underneath.

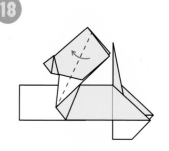

Fold the 18 line and tuck inside the head.

19

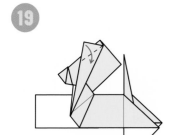

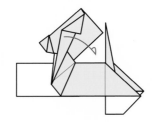

Fold line 19 forward, flattening the side of the head and tucking fold 18 inside. Repeat steps 18 and 19 on the other side.

20

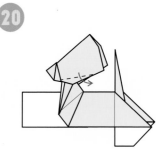

Fold the 20 lines forward, tucking the flaps inside.

21

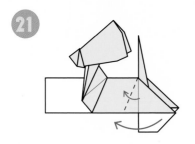

Fold the 21 lines forward, refolding the 10 lines.

22

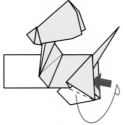

Open up the space between the back legs and fold line 22 forward, tucking against the base of the tail. Collapse the legs back together.

23

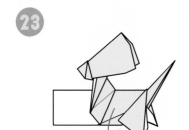

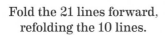

Fold the 23 lines.

24

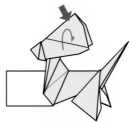

Fold the 24 lines, collapsing the top downward.

25

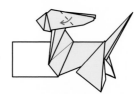

Fold the 25 lines forward.

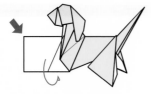

Fold the 26 lines and tuck into the chest area. Make sure this fold is slightly shorter and buries inside.

Crease along the edge and fold forward as shown.

Fold along the edge and fold forward as shown.

Fold the tips of each leg forward to create a foot.

CAT LEVEL ★★★☆

Does your city have a resident black cat, who roams from backyard to backyard? Or maybe there's an orange tabby that lives at the library (page 87). Wherever they live, fold these cats to give the residents of your city some feline friends! **Number of Folding Papers: 1**

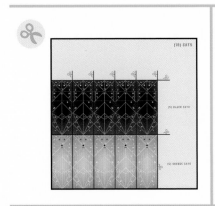

1

Fold line 1 back and unfold.

2

Fold and unfold line 2.

3

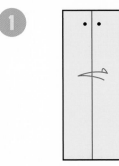 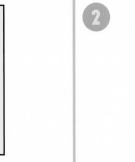 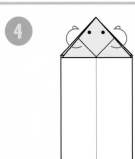

Fold the 3 lines back. Refold line 2 and collapse the model as shown. Flip the model over.

4

Fold the 4 lines back and tuck behind the head.

143

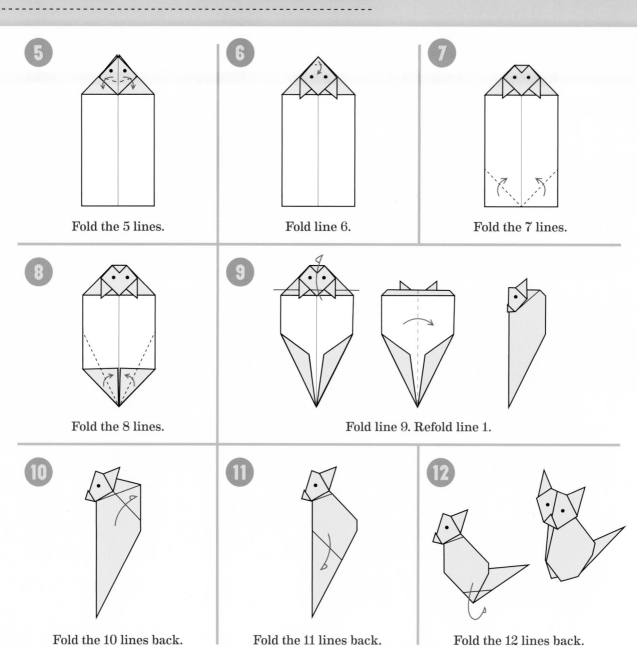

5 Fold the 5 lines.

6 Fold line 6.

7 Fold the 7 lines.

8 Fold the 8 lines.

9 Fold line 9. Refold line 1.

10 Fold the 10 lines back.

11 Fold the 11 lines back.

12 Fold the 12 lines back.

CHIPMUNK LEVEL ★★★★

Every city needs a little wildlife. Chipmunks are an adorable city-dwelling animal. They build nests in street trees, bury acorns in parks, and even root through trash cans for scraps of food! Where do the chipmunks make their homes in your city?

Number of Folding Papers: 1

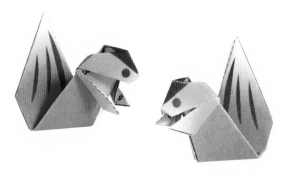

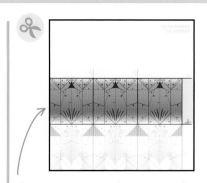

There are multiple projects on this folding paper. Cut out the chipmunk.

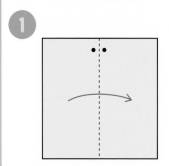

Fold line 1.

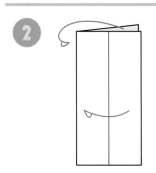

Fold the 2 lines back on both sides.

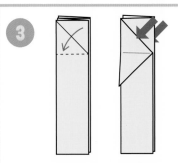

Fold and unfold the 3 lines, collapsing the model on both sides as shown.

Fold the 4 lines.

145

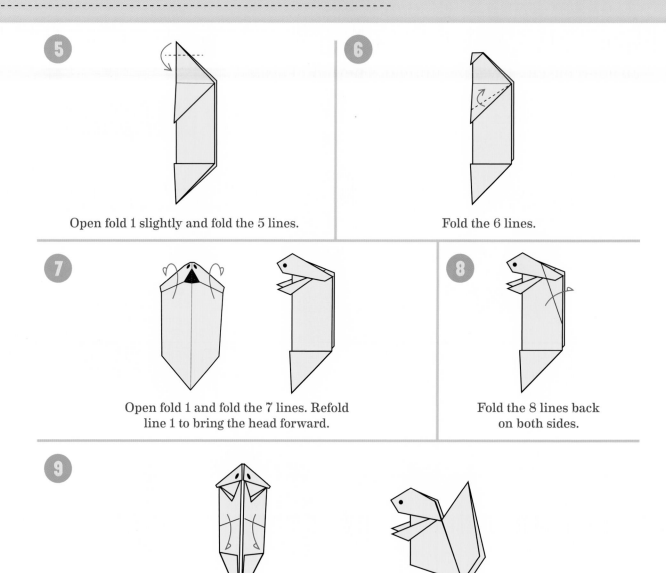

5 Open fold 1 slightly and fold the 5 lines.

6 Fold the 6 lines.

7 Open fold 1 and fold the 7 lines. Refold line 1 to bring the head forward.

8 Fold the 8 lines back on both sides.

9 Open fold 1 to face front. Fold the 9 lines back, collapsing the model as shown.

RABBIT LEVEL ⭐⭐⭐⭐

Rabbits make cute pets, but they also live in the wild. You might find them in the park, burrowed underground, or in nests well-hidden behind bushes (page 136). Once you learn to fold this one, get ready to fold a lot more because rabbits have very large families! **Number of Folding Papers: 1**

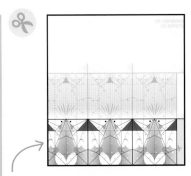

There are multiple projects on this folding paper. Cut out the rabbit.

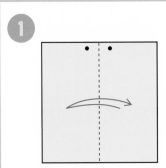

Fold and unfold line 1.

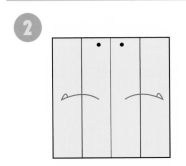

Fold the 2 lines back.

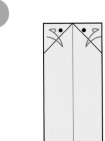

Fold the 3 lines back and unfold.

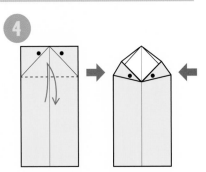

Fold and unfold line 4. Collapse the 3 lines as shown.

5

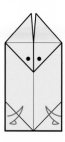

Fold the 5 lines back
and unfold.

6

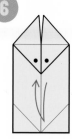

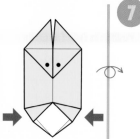

Fold and unfold line 6.
Collapse the 5 lines as shown.
Flip the model over.

7

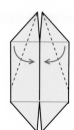

Fold the 7 lines.

8

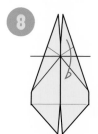

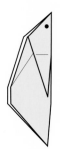

Fold line 8 back, then refold line 1.

9

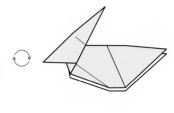
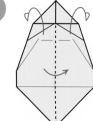

Unfold line 1 slightly to fold the 9 lines back.
Refold line 1 and rotate the model.

10

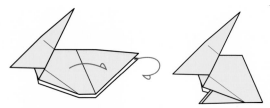

Fold the 10 lines back.

11

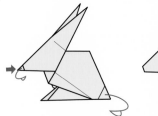
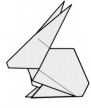

Fold the 11 lines back, collapsing
the nose, as shown.

About the Author

Taro Yaguchi is the founder of Taro's Origami Studio. By profession, he is a Japanese patent attorney, with offices in Tokyo and Philadelphia. Like all Japanese children, Taro started folding origami at a young age. However, it wasn't until he was an adult that origami became his passion. His first original design was a paper airplane, folded with a sheet of paper from his patent firm. He began experimenting with new folds on the many long transpacific flights his business requires him to take. Now Taro has his own studio with two locations in the United States and dozens of original designs ranging from cars and trucks to animals to buildings. Taro's Origami Studio has partnered with companies and brands like Louis Vuitton, Lexus, MetLife, Chase, ABC, Lord & Taylor, Conrad Hotels & Resorts, Nickelodeon, and Uniqlo, among others. Taro is currently developing an innovative origami teaching method and software for the best learning experience at his studio.

About the Illustrator

Simon Arizpe is an award-winning paper engineer and illustrator based in Brooklyn who has created books for Robert Sabuda, designed stationery for MoMA, and worked on various projects with Google, Disney, DC Comics, Paramount Pictures, and Hasbro Toys along the way. He is a professor of paper engineering and three-dimensional design at Pratt Institute and Parsons School of Design in New York City.